Balsamico!

Balsamico!

A Balsamic Vinegar Cookbook

Text & Recipes by Pamela Sheldon Johns

Produced by Jennifer Barry Design

Photography by Richard Jung

Ten Speed Press
Berkeley, California

A Kirsty Melville Book

Ten Speed Press
Box 7123, Berkeley, California 94707
www.tenspeed.com

Distributed in Australia by Simon & Schuster Australia, in New Zealand by Tandem Press,
in South Africa by Real Books, and in the United Kingdom and Europe by Airlift Books.

Concept and Design: Jennifer Barry Design, Sausalito, California
Design Assistant: Leslie Barry
Production Assistant: Kristen Wurz
Copy Editor: Carolyn Miller
Food Stylist: Pouké
Prop Stylist: Carol Hacker/Tableprop

Library of Congress Cataloging-in-Publication Data
Johns, Pamela Sheldon, 1953–
Balsamico! : a balsamic vinegar cookbook / text & recipes by Pamela Sheldon Johns :
produced by Jennifer Barry Design : photography by Richard Jung.
p.   cm.
Includes bibliographical references and index.
ISBN 1-58008-030-8 (alk. paper)
1. Cookery (Vinegar)   2. Balsamic vinegar.   I. Title.
TX819.v5J64   1999
641.6'2--dc21   98-27253   CIP

Printed in Hong Kong

First printing, 1999

1 2 3 4 5 6 7 8 9 10 — 03 02 01 00 99

Contents

Introduction

On the back of my hand rests a glistening drop of history, of tradition: *un miracolo*, a miracle, as the Italians call it. It warms on my skin, so viscous that it rises, clinging tightly, and sends aromatic messages to my nose. I inhale, and the centuries speak to me: tones of dark grape essence, sweet wood, and a trace of nose-tingling acidity. In the filtered light of the *acetaia,* the ancient attic where balsamic vinegar is aged, I raise my hand to taste the precious substance. It glides over my tongue and I taste simultaneously sweetness and a tinge of acidity. The honeylike consistency keeps it long in my mouth, and as I exhale, I can taste the wood: oak, cherry, and juniper. Lingering notes of port and cherry flirt with my senses. When I at last open my eyes, it is to see the satisfied, smiling face of a man who knew that a taste of his 150-year-old condiment would transport my taste buds to paradise.

Condiment is the best term for traditionally

made balsamic vinegar, known in Italy as Aceto Balsamico Tradizionale. It seems a shame to call it vinegar, for the process is quite different from that of making conventional wine vinegars. Nonetheless, it does go through an acetification process, and strictly speaking, is a vinegar. In the simplest terms, its making can be described as a long fermentation process that begins with grape must, the skin and pulp of fresh grapes, condensed by simmering it gently over an open fire for hours. It is then aged in a series of barrels of a variety of woods in light, airy attics for at least twelve years. The concentration in cooking and the evaporative aging process result in a thick, sweet vinegar. This age-old technique yields a singular product, that once tasted cannot be confused with any other.

Yet, there is confusion. Due to a great world-market demand, many counterfeits have appeared. Legal issues and promotional strategies

have clouded the distinction between the different grades of balsamic vinegar. Pricing and packaging can be wildly diverse, with no correlation to quality.

The dilemma for producers is that all balsamic vinegars not made in the traditional way must be labeled Aceto Balsamico di Modena, a designation that legally allows the addition of wine vinegar, caramel flavoring, and caramel coloring. This presents a problem, because the minimum standard required for Aceto Balsamico di Modena, also referred to as "industrial" grade, can result in an inferior product. It leaves a gap for the producer who makes a vinegar with integrity, that is, not using any additives, using quality ingredients, and aging in wood, but for a shorter time than prescribed for traditional balsamic vinegar. It is a problem especially for the producers of traditional balsamico, because there are so many vinegars making claims that simply cannot match the process and investment that goes into making the true Aceto Balsamico Tradizionale.

History

There isn't much documentation of the methods and uses of balsamic vinegar prior to the early eighteenth century. However, cooked grape must as a culinary ingredient is described by culinary historian Apicius in the first century. *Agrodolce*, or sweet and sour sauce, also called *saba*, was made by the Romans with cooked and reduced grapes. Still used with desserts and polenta, *agrodolce* is created with filtered white wine must boiled down to one-third its original volume. Some speculate that some *agrodolce* was originally a happy accident of natural fermentation. Perhaps a very tart vinegar may have been moderated with *agrodolce*. According to Renato Bergonzini, professor and author of several books on the subject of *aceto balsamico*, the nobility made *agrodolce* for five to six centuries.

Although we may never know the precise origins of aceto balsamico, there are stories about similar substances. One favorite legend tells of an incident in 1046 when Arrigo III, on his way to Rome to be crowned emperor, requested a gift of a special vinegar he had heard of. The gift came from the Marquis of Canossa Bonifacio in the current territory of Reggio Emilia. Was it balsamic vinegar? Certainly, an 1100 description of a similar product called *balsamo*, or balm, fits the essence of aceto balsamico; it was used only for medicinal purposes, although there were rumors of its aphrodisiac qualities. From the twelfth to the fourteenth centuries, a product of a similar nature was made, and consortia were formed to keep the production of this special vinegar a secret.

In 1502, the duke of Ferrara, Alfonso I d'Este, married Lucrezia Borgia. Modena was the capital of the Estense *ducale*, and the Este family built for themselves an *acetaia* in what is now the military academy. In 1581, Ludovico Mitterpacher, a Hungarian journalist and agricultural scholar, wrote at length about the process of making a sweet vinegar in Modena. The elaborate technique involved the insertion of a burning brick into the mixture and the aging in mulberry wood barrels of decreasing size for six years. It did not, however, start with cooked grape must, but simply with pressed grapes.

Napoleon's presence in Modena temporarily ended the reign of the Estes, and the famous *acetaia* was auctioned away. In the Este family records there are many references to *aceto balsamico*, as gifts to important foreign rulers, and especially in the dowry lists of the noblewomen. It was probably during this period that it came into use as a gastronomic component, from sipping it as a digestive, to drizzling it as a condiment. Documents of the time clearly differentiate between vinegars that were used for cooking, as a condiment, and for sipping.

Bits and pieces of documentation, such as a letter from the village of Nonantola in 1839 that talked about 130-year-old barrels, continued to confirm the existence of a uniquely aged vinegar. A well-documented description of how balsamic vinegar was made in 1862 was written in a letter by Sir Francesco Aggazzotti. At this time, the definition and science of balsamic vinegar became generally understood.

A new history of aceto balsamico began in the late 1970s, with major exports to other European countries and the United States. A continuing trend with chefs, balsamic vinegar has now become a household word, with bottles sporting the name on every supermarket shelf. In order for consumers to understand what they are buying, it is important to be aware of where and how both traditional and industrial balsamic vinegars are made.

Zona Tipica

The *zona tipica* is the legally identified area in which a product can be made. This delineation can be compared to winemaking D.O.C. zones, or the Denominazione di Origine Controllata (denomination of controlled origin), which not only controls the geographic origin of specific wines, but also outlines permitted ingredients and defines the production and aging process.

The region of Emilia-Romagna is bounteous in exceptional traditional products. The fertile land surrounding Modena, Parma, and Reggio Emilia, and the inspiration of producers there, have created foods that are recognized the world over: Parmigiano-Reggiano, Lambrusco wine, prosciutto di Parma, *nocino* (walnut liqueur), Vignola cherries, and *zampone* (a cooked pork sausage stuffed into a pig's leg), to name the most familiar.

Balsamic vinegar is part of this heritage, with two zones specified for the production of traditional balsamic vinegar: the provinces of Modena and Reggio Emilia. Born of the same noble roots, the region for production split when the two provinces were divided at Italy's unification in 1862. In general, the two traditional balsamic vinegars follow the same prescribed law for production, but some differences can be detected. For example, in the past, only Reggio Emilia used juniper barrels as a component of aging, while Modena preferred mulberry. In Reggio Emilia, the grape must was cooked for a shorter time, resulting in a less-sweet, more pungent vinegar. But today practices have become more universal. The major difference now is in the controls used in evaluating and guaranteeing the product by the individual consortia. Modena is much larger, and more organized, whereas the smaller Reggio Emilia Consorzio, while quite serious, has taken criticism for lax controls. It is always a matter of taste for the consumer, and the only way to judge the difference is to try each for yourself.

Of course, with the huge demand for balsamic vinegar, there are imitators outside the *zona tipica* who are trying to create a comparable product. In Chianti, Umbria, and Naples; in the California counties of Sonoma and Napa; in Germany and elsewhere, individuals are following a similar process for making an aged vinegar from cooked grape must. It will never be the same as the original, though, because the climate, grapes, and general ambiance of this part of Emilia-Romagna cannot be reproduced.

Visits to Typical Acetaie

Aceto balsamico has such simple beginnings—how does it become such a complex end product? Every traditional balsamic vinegar starts with the same essentials: grapes, barrels, and time-honored traditions. Variations in each of these components affect the final outcome, but the core process is always the same.

Grapes

By law, only locally grown grapes of specific varieties can be used: Trebbiano, Occhio di Gatto, Spergola, Berzemino, and Lambrusco. By far, the favored grape is the white Trebbiano. A clone also prized is the Trebbiano di Spagna, a sweet, low-yield grape that

grows best on rolling hills. The grapes are picked when quite ripe and are processed almost immediately, before fermentation can begin.

Barrels

The barrels for making balsamic vinegar range in size from 10 to 75 liters, depending on the number of barrels in a sequence. This sequence is called a battery. The typical battery consists of three or more barrels, with a special rectangular opening at the top to permit the addition and removal of vinegar, to allow visual inspection and tasting, and to provide necessary contact with the air. This opening is lightly covered with gauze or a similar material to prevent foreign matter from falling in. The barrels rest on their sides in a notched wooden rack, placed in graduating order by size. Continuing the work of generations of master barrel coopers, Modena's Francesco Renzi, like his own ancestors, handcrafts these barrels with extra-thick staves to last for many generations.

Aceto balsamico is most often is aged in oak from Slavonia and Croatia, chestnut from Alto Veneto, and Italian acacia, ash, and wild cherry. The most precious woods, and most difficult to find, are juniper and mulberry. Occasionally a custom barrel will be made with ends, or heads, of these prized woods to allow the aceto balsamico to absorb their distinct and pungent essence. Preferences in wood vary from producer to producer. Often an *acetaia* will have only one juniper barrel, which is used for

IT TAKES A YEAR
JUST TO PREPARE NEW
BARRELS FOR THE
PRODUCTION OF
ACETO BALSAMICO.
FIRST THEY ARE
RINSED WITH BOILING
SALTED WATER,
THEN BOILING WINE
VINEGAR. THEN
THEY ARE FILLED
WITH WINE, WHICH
WILL TURN TO WINE
VINEGAR OVER
THE YEAR THAT IT
REMAINS. THIS
FERMENTATION
PROCESS INOCULATES
THE WOOD WITH
THE ACETOBACTER
NECESSARY TO
ACETIFY THE COOKED
MUST WHEN IT IS
FINALLY ADDED.

FRANCESCO RENZI
OF MODENA IS A
MASTER COOPER WHO
SPECIALIZES IN HAND-
CRAFTED BARRELS FOR
ACETO BALSAMICO.
THE WOOD AGES
NATURALLY OUTSIDE
FOR FOUR TO FIVE
YEARS BEFORE IT
BEGINS ITS
TRANSFORMATION TO
A BARREL. AFTER
SOAKING, THE WOOD
IS LEFT TO BEND INTO
SHAPE FOR THREE
MONTHS. THE
BARRELS ARE FORMED
BY HAND WITH STAVES
THAT ARE EXTRA-
THICK, TO LAST FOR
GENERATIONS. EACH
BARREL IS THEN
STAMPED WITH THE
NAME OF THE NEW
OWNER, NEXT TO THE
BURNED-BRAND
TRADEMARK OF THE
RENZI FAMILY.

A VARIETY OF WOODS ARE USED FOR ACETO BALSAMICO TRADIZIONALE BARRELS. SOME PROVIDE AROMATIC CONTRIBUTIONS, OTHERS ARE IMPORTANT FOR THEIR HARDNESS AND THE ABILITY TO CONCENTRATE THE AGING VINEGAR. JUNIPER IS ESPECIALLY PRIZED FOR THE UNIQUE FLAVOR IT IMPARTS. ACACIA AND ASH WERE NOT USED HISTORICALLY, BUT HAVE BEEN ADDED IN MODERN TIMES WITH GREAT SUCCESS.

ROVERE/OAK
CASTAGNO/CHESTNUT
ROBINIA/ACACIA
FRASSINO/ASH
CILIEGIO/CHERRY
GINEPRO/JUNIPER
GELSO/MULBERRY

blending. The qualities of each wood influence the aceto balsamico in different ways: chestnut is rich in tannin and gives good color; cherry is sweet; and oak, because of its density, helps to concentrate the vinegar and is often used in the first and last barrels of the sequence.

Renzi starts with raw wood, which ages naturally outside for four to five years. It is then soaked and is bent into shape over a period of three months. In mid-September, when the weather is humid, the wood is brought in. The precision work of barrel crafting is done by hand by Renzi's sons, Matteo and Roberto. They make over 800,000 barrels a year, customizing each one with the customer's surname next to their stamp, "F. Renzi, Modena." The type of wood is also stamped on the head.

Barrels that have been in families for centuries often begin to leak. The years of balsamic sediment and culture in the barrel is much too precious to lose, so Renzi is often called on to craft a new barrel around an ancient one. This practice allows the vinegar to remain in contact with generations of vinegars, one of the essential elements in a high-quality aceto balsamico. The craftsmanship involved in creating the new barrel requires great skill to be sure that the fit is snug and will last many generations more.

It takes a year just to prepare new barrels for the production of aceto balsamico. First they are filled with boiling salted water and left for two days to remove the tannin from the woods. The saltwater is rinsed away, and the barrel filled again with boiling wine vinegar. The barrels are then emptied and filled with wine that will turn to wine vinegar over the year that it remains in the barrel. This fermentation process inoculates the wood with the acetobacter necessary to acetify the cooked must when it is finally added. The barrel is once again rinsed with wine vinegar and placed in the attic, ready to accept the cooked grape must that will become balsamic vinegar. The barrels are never again completely filled or emptied, and at least 25 percent of the barrel is left unfilled for air space.

Time-Honored Traditions:
Cooking the Grape Must

In early October, Mariangela Montanari met me at the tenth-century Castello Vignola. From the guard tower we had a panoramic view of Vignola and the Panaro River, looking over cherry orchards that must be exquisite in spring.

Through Vignola and into the countryside we arrived by a small dirt road to the family *acetaia*, Mariangela's great-grandfather Alfonso's

1893 stone-walled farmhouse, La Ca' dal Non' (Grandfather's House). Her friend Pier Paolo Bortolotti was unloading large baskets of Trebbiano di Spagna grapes, while her brother Michele was hard at work at the *mostatrice*, a machine that removes the stems. Inside, her father Vittorio was watching over the cooking of the freshly pressed grape must.

Mariangela explains the importance of the close-knit relationship of family and friends: "Our aim is to carry on the culture of traditional balsamic vinegar of Modena and to spread it beyond its historical borders, all over the world. It is a beautiful business for us because we can all stay together." Mechanical engineer Vittorio sees it as a revived hobby and a future business for his children. Pier Paolo is studying the scientific art of making aceto balsamico at the university and brings his expertise to the business. The marketing and business aspects are left to Mariangela and Michele.

In the past, the cooking was done in copper vats over wood fires, but today most producers use stainless steel over an open gas flame. While copper's natural properties enhance the release of sugars, the stainless steel provides a more even cooking surface. A thermostat controls the temperature so that the grapes will not burn, but slowly condense and concentrate the natural sugars. The first thirty minutes, they cook at 195° to 200°F, then the temperature is lowered to 175° to 185°F for 24 to 36 hours. The vats are open to induce evaporation and reduction of the grape must; after at least 24 hours it will be half of the original volume and have a sugar content of 20 to 24 percent.

Following this lengthy cooking period, the mixture is left in a large wooden cask for a couple of months to begin its fermentation. The first metabolic changes occur as the sugar transforms into alcohol, precipitated by natural yeasts in the grapes. This is followed by an oxidation by acetobacters that changes the alcohol into acetic acid and turns the must to vinegar. Once this process has begun, the mixture can be put into the battery of wood barrels. As it ages, the acetic acids and alcohol diminish, yet the taste remains lively and mellow at the same time.

A slow alcoholic fermentation is desired, and the climate helps to control that. In the winter months that follow, the mixture has a chance to settle, allowing the solid particles to form and thus clarify the vinegar. In the next and subsequent summers, as the air heats up, so does the fermentation activity, only to slow down and rest in the cooler months. The optimum exposure to the elements has been found to be in uninsulated attics. With the barrels open to the air, evaporation continues the reduction and concentration processes.

Aging

Quietly dwelling in a simple country house in the countryside north of Modena is one of the area's largest producers of traditional aceto balsamico. Originally the *acetaia* of the recently deceased Loris Bellei, a well-known grand master of balsamic vinegar, Acetaia del Cristo is now owned by Eugenio and Giorgio Barbieri, with assistance from expert vinegar-maker Otello Bonfatti. With over 1,000 barrels, they generate 3,000 to 3,500 bottles of traditional vinegar per year. Even with that amount of production, they are still only using 1 to 2 percent of the vinegar aging in barrels. All of the grapes are estate-grown in this area famous for Lambrusco. The organization of the *acetaia* is interesting and different, with barrels arranged by like sizes instead of in graduating sizes. All of the barrels of one size are grouped together, perhaps to save space. In the tasting room, Barbieri and his daughter Erika point out that only Consorzio-approved vinegars are made here, with minimum ages of twelve and twenty-five years. They brought out a sample of a unique balsamico variation that met these standards, a twenty-five-year-old vinegar aged only in cherry wood that made my mouth sing.

Every barrel is open, but covered lightly with simple woven cotton cloths to block the entry of flying insects. Historically, some producers used rocks from the Panaro River. The acetification in the barrel caused these particular rocks to form calcium deposits. It was a sign that things were progressing nicely in the barrel.

Ermes Malpighi's *acetaia* is in his home, just on the outskirts of Modena. After passing through his neatly manicured gardens replete with black and white swans, I entered the *acetaia*; immediately I sensed the aromas of ancient blends. The barrels have been painted a uniform black, increasing the drama of the attic. Each barrel opening is covered neatly

EUGENIO BARBIERI
AND OTELLO
BONFATTI WITHDRAW
A SAMPLE OF
ACETO BALSAMICO
TRADIZIONALE.

ACETAIA DEL CRISTO,
SAN PROSPERO

by linen cloths with handmade lace edging done by his mother. Malpighi gave me a lesson on the five components of making aceto balsamico: the *zona tipica*, the grapes, the influence of the climate, the barrels, and the passion. Perhaps the one element he didn't mention was patience. Malpighi produces 4,000 bottles of ivory- and gold-label balsamico a year from approximately 520 barrels. "After twenty-five years, 70 to 90 kilograms [154 to 198 pounds] of grapes will yield just over seven bottles of *extravecchio* [extra old] *balsamico*, aged at least twenty-five years. That kind of reduction results in a great investment in many ways, but especially an investment of time."

Thirty kilometers outside of Modena, in the rolling hills and forests above Sassuolo, is the pristine grand *acetaia* of Sante Bertoni with over 1,500 barrels, including some very old barrels from Germany and Sicily. Stretching the definition of *tradizionale* to its limits, Bertoni has been able to produce a high-quality balsamic vinegar in less than the usual time. Labeled a rebel by some, a revolutionary by others, he has confounded the expert tasters by bringing in extremely high scores for relatively young vinegars. He starts with his estate-grown Trebbiano and Lambrusco Grasparossa grapes, gently cooked for twenty-four hours in the typical way to a sugar content of about 30 percent. Bertoni's variation in technique is in the starting fermentation. Instead of immediately introducing the cooked must to a battery of barrels, he lets it rest in glass for two months. It is then transferred to large oak casks and blended 50 percent with previously aged vinegar to begin a slow fermentation for one year. After passing another year in smaller oak barrels, it has already converted to vinegar before being introduced to a battery of barrels. This kick-start takes precious time off the total aging process to reach an equally tasty end product.

Transferring and Topping Off
This essential process takes place in winter, usually between September and March, depending on when the new batch of cooked must will be added. The primary factor is that it occurs when

the weather is cool and fermentation is slow.

In Magreta, at the very edge of Modena province where the River Secchia borders Reggio Emilia, is a charming farm and ancient *acetaia* that dates back to 1871. The ambiance at Giovanni Leonardi's *acetaia* is like stepping back in time. A veritable antique museum of tools and farm implements, the *acetaia* also is home to some very old barrels, one with the stamp of Mathilde, of the noble Canossa family. Dodging cats, dogs, and peacocks, I step inside the barn and bend over to climb the wooden stairs to the attic to observe the ritual of transferring the aceto balsamico from barrel to barrel.

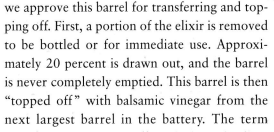

The process begins with the smallest barrel of the battery, which is presumably where the aceto balsamico has reached the point of greatest aging. Giovanni and his daughter Clara use a "thief" to remove a sample for tasting. We all receive drops on the back of our hands to test. First, the color and viscosity is examined, then the aroma, and finally we taste it. The aceto balsamico is aromatic and very fine, and

we approve this barrel for transferring and topping off. First, a portion of the elixir is removed to be bottled or for immediate use. Approximately 20 percent is drawn out, and the barrel is never completely emptied. This barrel is then "topped off" with balsamic vinegar from the next largest barrel in the battery. The term *topping off* is a little misleading, as the barrels are never actually filled to the top, just replenished to 75 percent capacity. The step is repeated for each barrel until the open space is left in the last, and largest, barrel. This is where the new cooked must will be added.

In addition to traditional balsamic vinegar, the Leonardi *acetaia* also produces a number of high-quality balsamic vinegars, all of which are aged in wood from three to thirty years. They also bottle and sell *saba*, highly reduced grape must that has not been fermented or aged.

Among the various *acetaie*, there are subtle differences. Some producers cook their must longer; some introduce the cooked must immediately into the battery; and as you can see,

GIOVANNI LEONARDI
PERFORMS THE
OPERATIONS OF
TRANSFERRING AND
TOPPING OFF.
CLOCKWISE FROM
UPPER LEFT: A SAMPLE
OF THIRTY-YEAR-OLD
ACETO BALSAMICO
IS WITHDRAWN
FROM THE LAST AND
SMALLEST BARREL
TO BE TASTED.
AFTER REMOVING A
PORTION FROM THE
SMALLEST BARREL TO
BE BOTTLED, VINEGAR
FROM THE NEXT
LARGEST BARREL IS
REMOVED AND USED
TO TOP OFF THE VOID.
THIS PROCESS IS
REPEATED UNTIL THE
EMPTY SPACE IS IN THE
LARGEST BARREL OF
THE BATTERY. THIS IS
WHERE THE NEW
COOKED MUST WILL
BE ADDED.

ACETAIA LEONARDI,
MAGRETA

ACETO BALSAMICO
TRADIZIONALE

─────────

COLOR: DARK
BROWN, FULL OF
WARMTH AND LIGHT
DENSITY: FLUID,
BUT THICK
AROMA: COMPLEX,
WITH TONES OF
WOOD AND GRAPES
FLAVOR: RICH, SWEET,
AND SOUR, ALL
PERFECTLY
PROPORTIONED

ACETO BALSAMICO
DI MODENA

─────────

COLOR: DARK BROWN
DENSITY: THIN
AND WATERY
AROMA: WINE
VINEGAR AND SUGAR
FLAVOR: ACIDIC, WITH
CARAMEL AFTERTASTE

some have different methods of aging. Every bottle of traditional balsamic vinegar is different, not only among different producers, but even from a single producer. Each year a battery of barrels yields a unique product. Because the barrels are never completely emptied, each barrel is a new blend, with traces of aceto balsamico that date back to the origins of the barrel's first batch of cooked must.

In 1962 the law changed to permit the production and sale of balsamic vinegar made with cooked grape must. This could describe a traditional aceto balsamico, but the wording was not specific enough to prevent some producers from finding less expensive ways to meet the growing demand for balsamic vinegar. Products found their way onto the market that had only a percentage of cooked and aged must, just enough to satisfy the letter of the law. Producers of the traditional aceto balsamico raised enough objections that on December 3, 1965, a generic rule was created to define the zone of production for an industrial product called Aceto Balsamico di Modena.

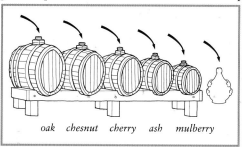

oak   chesnut   cherry   ash   mulberry

The definition of Aceto Balsamico di Modena is so loosely written that there can be a wide range of quality from producer to producer. One reputable company is Cavalli in Scandiano, Reggio Emilia. The late Ferdinando Cavalli began collecting barrels in 1920 from old vinegar factories and estates that belonged to the noble families of Reggio Emilia, some dating back to the early eighteenth century. Cavalli turned a personal hobby of creating award-winning traditional balsamic vinegar into a business in 1980 and became the founder of the Consorzio for traditional balsamic vinegar in Reggio Emilia. He began producing industrial balsamic vinegar in the late sixties, maintaining the important steps of using cooked grape must and aging in wood.

Today his sons Roberto and Giovanni continue the business. In addition to an excellent traditional balsamic vinegar, they make their own wine vinegar to add to their "semi-balsamico," a condiment made with cooked must and kept in oak for two to three years. To export 40,000 bottles a year to the United

States, they process over 1 million pounds of grapes a year.

That is an astounding figure until you compare it to another producer I visited. In a modern facility with highly automated labeling, dating, and casing, this industrial giant is putting out 2,700 bottles an hour and exporting over 15 million liters of Aceto Balsamico di Modena a year. The grape requirement for this magnitude of industrial vinegar is over 88 million pounds a year.

In this factory, most of the vinegar goes directly into glass, although one level of product spends a year in massive oak barrels as big as cars. It is questionable if the vinegar can really be influenced by the wood when it is in such volume and never stirred.

The Consorzie

Three groups have formed to protect and support the production of traditional balsamic vinegar made in the time-honored way. The Consorteria in Spilamberto has become a sort of spiritual mother to the other two, providing inspiration as well as training to the master tasters. The other two groups represent the two regions making traditional balsamic vinegar, Modena and Reggio Emilia.

The Consorteria dell'Aceto Balsamico Tradizionale di Modena (Spilamberto)

In 1967, the Consorteria di Spilamberto was established. Their aim was to study and evaluate the tradition of making Aceto Balsamico Tradizionale and to clearly define the difference between the industrial vinegar and the traditional vinegar.

Consorteria literally translates to "coterie," or "brotherhood." The *consorteria* was founded by Rolando Simonini and now has more than 1,500 members. For over a decade they have sponsored the master taster courses required to certify the experts who guarantee the product. The master course takes at least nine years to pass, consisting of twelve theoretical lessons and exams, a two-year tasting exam, and three years of solo tasting at a staggering one hundred tastings per year. Throughout the course, students earn the title of apprentice taster, taster, and ultimately master taster.

The twelve members of the board of directors, headed this year by Francesco Saccani, advise and devote themselves to protecting the culture of traditional balsamic vinegar. This organization is also responsible for creating the tasting evaluation form utilized by the Consorzio.

Every year, producers anxiously await the Palio di San Giovanni on June 24, the dual observance of the birth of Saint John the Baptist, patron saint of love and friendship, and Midsummer's Eve. Historically, this is a time of celebrating summer's bounty, when traditional bonfires are lit to symbolize the strength of the summer sun. Over 1,000 samples of traditional balsamic vinegar are presented in competition for the grand award, the best aceto balsamico of the year.

The Consorzio of Producers of Traditional Balsamic Vinegar of Modena

Modena's consortium was founded in 1979 to "promote and defend the production of Traditional Balsamic Vinegar of Modena." Its offices are currently housed in the Palazzo Guidotti, home of its first president and also the location of the Antiche Acetaia of Count Guidotti Bentivoglio, one of the oldest *acetaie* in Modena, dating back to the fifteenth century. The function of the Consorzio today is to legally represent producers, and to control and guarantee the testing of samples, the performance of the bottling, and the application of the quality seal, which is the guarantee that the aceto balsamico meets all qualifications set forth by law. All members pay 200,000 lire (approximately $125) a year to belong to the Consorzio. This entitles them to the privilege of evaluation by master tasters and representation in legal battles. Of the roughly 120 members, only 25 percent bottle to sell; the others make balsamico strictly for their own use and for gifts.

Approximately 20,000 bottles a year pass testing and are bottled, sealed, and numbered in the unique 100-ml bottle designed by Giorgetto Giugiaro, also a renowned car designer. The short, stocky bottle, a round globe bottom on its own glass stand, is labeled on one side by the Consorzio, and on the other side by the producer. A gold capsule is placed over the cork of vinegar that has aged twenty-five years or more; an ivory capsule designates a minimum of twelve years in barrels. The colored capsules are not a legal distinction, but offer a quick identification of the younger and more aged aceto balsamico. Covering the color-coded capsule, is a seal, a paper strip with the words *Aceto Balsamico Tradizionale di Modena D.O.C.* on the left side. In the center, and on the very top of the bottle, is the logo of an antique jar on an orange background. On the right side, are the words *Sigillo di garanzia Consorzio Produttori* (Seal of guarantee of the Consorzio of Producers), along with an individual serial number that relates to the sample, which was

"TRADITIONAL BALSAMIC VINEGAR IS PRODUCED IN THE AREA OF THE ANCIENT LANDS OF THE DUCAL FAMILY OF ESTE. WITH NO ADDITION OF ANY AROMATIC SUBSTANCES, IT IS OBTAINED FROM COOKED GRAPE MUST MATURED THROUGH SLOW ACETIFICATION FOR NATURAL FERMENTATION AND PROGRESSIVE CONCENTRATION BY MEANS OF A VERY LONG AGING IN A SET OF VESSELS OF DIFFERENT KINDS OF WOOD. OF A DEEP, DARK, AND GLIMMERING BROWN COLOR, AN APPROPRIATE SMOOTHNESS AND THICKNESS SHOW ITS DENSITY. ITS INIMITABLE WELL-BALANCED SWEET AND SOUR TASTE ALLOWS ITSELF TO BE GENEROUSLY FULL, SAPID, AND WITH DOWNY NUANCES IN ACCORDANCE WITH ITS OWN OLFACTORY NATURE."

—THE TASTE MASTERS, SPILAMBERTO, 1976

tested under very strict conditions. In addition to the annual membership fee, producers pay for this bottling—approximately $8 for each ivory-capped twelve-year-old vinegar and around $14 for the gold-capped *extravecchio*.

When ready for evaluation, producers bring their product to the Consorzio in sealed containers. Samples are placed in 10-cc vials. When samples from six producers have accumulated, five tasters are given a two-day notice to show up. The samples to be tasted are anonymous, and the tasters do not know who will be in attendance until they arrive. These rotating tasters are from a pool of over thirty experts who have been trained and certified by the Consorteria of Spilamberto.

The panel of five sit at the table with privacy panels separating them. Each carrel has a candle, a ceramic spoon, bread sticks, a glass of water, and a checklist. Each sample is scored individually on visual aspects, aroma, and flavor. When at last the privacy panels are removed, the scores are averaged and a roundtable discussion takes place about each

sample. Evaluators whose scores varied considerably from the majority must defend their assessment, and the final decision must be unanimous. It is surprising to see the uniformity in scoring. The minimum score from a possible 400 points for the ivory cap is 229; for the gold, or *extravecchio*, a minimum of 255 is required.

The final score is determined, and the sample passes— or doesn't.

Roughly half of the samples are returned to the producer for further aging and adjustment. From here, the approved aceto balsamico is put into the bottles by Consorzio personnel, under strict controls. The Consorzio label, printed with the logo and the definition of the *antico condimento*, is affixed on one side of the bottle, and the other side is free for the producer to personalize with his or her own label. The seal of guarantee on a paper strip is placed over the cork and colored capsule, individually numbered to correlate to the samples library kept in the Consorzio offices, which includes a sample of every specimen ever submitted for tasting.

Marco Costanzini runs the Consorzio almost single-handedly, spending a tremendous amount of time on the ongoing legal battle—which Italian culinary expert Faith Willinger has dubbed "the balsamic wars"—between Aceto Balsamico di Modena producers clocking in at a current 30 million bottles a year and the traditional producers with only 20 thousand bottles. He also is the watchdog for products that "imitate" Aceto Balsamico Tradizionale and don't fit into a legal category.

On March 4, 1986, the government finally recognized the D.O.C. of *Aceto Balsamico Tradizionale di Modena* and of *Aceto Balsamico Tradizionale di Reggio Emilia.*

This distinction led to the formation of a second consorzio in Reggio Emilia with essentially the same objective, to protect the traditional product.

The Consorzio of Producers of Traditional Balsamic Vinegar of Reggio Emilia

Founded by Ferdinando Cavalli in 1986 for the protection of traditional balsamic vinegar of Reggio Emilia, the Consortium (without any profit motive) has the aims of: "promoting any useful initiative for protecting the typicalness and characteristics of Traditional Balsamic Vinegar of Reggio Emilia, distinguishing and guaranteeing the product by means of special trademarks, assisting and advising the consortium members on improving production and commercialization, and lastly, control and supervision of production and commercialization."

Tasting is done by members of a technical committee who also act as consultants in the above goals. I had the unique opportunity to sit in on one of the tastings. On a Monday night in October, Giovanni Cavalli picked me up at my hotel in Reggio Emilia for a short drive to the local high school. We entered the chemistry lab and were greeted by the evening's testers. The room was set up against the background of the classroom's tubes and Bunsen burners. Five panels of five men each were ready to make very important decisions about the twenty-five samples of aceto balsamico on hand for testing.

As it turned out, the sixth panel was incomplete, with only two men, and since it was already set up for judging, I had the privilege to participate in the tasting. We held each sample up to the light of flashlights instead of candles, for they believe that this light is more consistent. Then we tasted. To me, they were all delicious; it was impossible to attach a numerical value to the extraordinary fireworks occurring in my taste buds, but the others were diligent, and proceeded to evaluate, average the scores, and discuss the outcomes. In addition to the visual aspects, they rated each sample on aroma, and finally, taste. Technically, the law only provides for two grades, twelve-year-old and twenty-five-year-old, but the Reggio Emilia producers have added a third level: red (traditional, twelve years old), silver (superior quality, 20 to 25 years old), or gold (*extravecchio*, 30 to 40 years old). The producers are then allowed to bottle in their own workshops and seal it with sealing wax. The 100-ml bottle is a tall, slender vase-like bottle with a visible cork that has been

sealed with red sealing wax. The Reggio Emilia Consorzio label is round with the logo made of the letters AB. Reggio Emilia also holds a yearly tasting competition called the Palio Mathilde. Recently, the judges have added a new tasting evaluation using the data from chemical analyses in addition to tasting.

In spite of the lobbying on the part of the Consorteria and the two *consorzie*, confusion reigned in the late eighties. The definition still called the traditional product *aceto*; it could only be sold as a vinegar. Work continued to redefine it as a condiment, a designation that would allow it to be sold as a commercial product in the world market. At last, on March 3, 1987, a ministerial decree established the standards for production and quality control, finally considering aceto balsamico a food condiment. Legally defined, in both provinces, the end product must be produced by these guidelines: It must be obtained from the must of specified local traditionally grown grapes, which are cooked on an open flame. Aging and refinement must take place in wooden casks numbering at least three over a period of at least twelve years.

Once again, crafty producers of the industrial product found a loophole and created blends using a small percentage of cooked musts that had aged the minimum period. To add to the confusion, the producers of industrial products started their own Consorzio per la Tutela di Aceto Balsamico di Modena.

Current legal battles are no less stupefying. Any product that falls between Aceto Balsamico di Modena and Aceto Balsamico Tradizionale di Modena or Reggio Emilia is essentially an illegal product. Counterfeits abound.

Buying Aceto Balsamico
There is no mistaking traditional balsamic vinegar from Modena and Reggio Emilia. Remember to look for each consortium's logo as described above.

Determining quality among industrial vinegars, or Aceto Balsamico di Modena, is trickier. "Aged in wood" can mean many things. Unless the length of aging is specified, it could simply mean that all or even just part of the vinegar stood in wood for as little as a month. Often wood chips are added to the aging vin-

egar to provide some of the aroma associated with traditional vinegars. Sometimes the wood barrels are so large that it is questionable if the vinegar in the middle of the barrel ever has contact with the wood. Price may give you some indication, but consider the beauty of the packaging in the price. Read the ingredients—if the product was made with cooked must, it will say so. If it has caramel coloring or flavoring added, it should state that as well.

It is not unusual to find "balsamic vinegar" that has been bottled in the United States; it is likely not the best quality. The list of ingredients only says that it contains "balsamic vinegar of Modena," rather than listing the individual ingredients, a devious way to avoid talking about additives. Exported bottles will identify where the vinegar was bottled by an API (*Aceti Produzione Imbottigliamento* or where the vinegar was bottled) code. Look for API MO for Modena vinegars and API RE for those from Reggio Emilia.

Storing Aceto Balsamico
Since traditional aceto balsamico is made in light and exposed to extreme temperatures, these elements will not necessarily damage it

later as you store it. Still, the best conditions are probably a cool, dark cupboard. Keep the bottle tightly closed and out of reach of anyone who doesn't understand exactly what it is.

Cooking with Aceto Balsamico

Flavor can vary from bottle to bottle of traditional aceto balsamico. Some are higher in acidity and enhance savory foods, while others are sweeter and woodier, excellent for desserts and after-dinner use. In any case, traditional aceto balsamico should be issued drop by drop. It is too precious to whisk into a salad dressing, unless you have your own *acetaia*! In a moment of extravagance, you might use it to flavor a mayonnaise, but the full taste of traditional aceto balsamico will be lost in such rich mediums. It shouldn't be cooked, but added only at the moment of serving.

The following recipes illustrate distinctly different uses for Aceto Balsamico di Modena and Aceto Balsamico Tradizionale. Some chefs recommend creating a substitute for traditional balsamic vinegar by reducing Aceto Balsamico di Modena over high heat until quite thick, and sometimes adding brown sugar. One must remember that most Aceto Balsamico di Modena has wine vinegar in it, and depending on the quality of the product, reducing it can be just like making a reduction of wine vinegar. In most cases, the result is too strong, too acidic, and light years away from the traditional product that you are seeking to imitate. If you are unable to get a good-quality Aceto Balsamico di Modena with little or no wine vinegar, don't try to fake it. Either use the traditional product or accept the difference in flavor with the industrial product.

Use Aceto Balsamico di Modena as you would a wine vinegar; in salads, as a marinade, and to brighten sauces. Try it as a condiment, also, tossed with grilled vegetables or pasta or drizzled over roasted meats. In general, don't use it in desserts.

The supreme use of traditional balsamic vinegar is as a table condiment, simply drizzled over any number of foods at any phase of the meal, or even taken as an after-dinner liqueur. One-half teaspoon per person is recommended per serving. As a condiment, use just enough to enhance the food it is served on, but not so much that it overpowers the other flavors.

Openers

Italian Vegetable Dipping Sauce

Traditionally, this dish, called pinzimonio, *is an assortment of seasonal vegetables arranged on a platter and served with small dishes of fruity, fresh extra-virgin olive oil, seasoned with salt and freshly ground pepper for dipping. Here, an additional condiment is added: balsamic vinegar!*

1 red bell pepper, seeded, deribbed, and cut into 1/2-inch-wide strips
3 carrots, peeled and cut lengthwise into 1/2-inch-wide strips
1 cucumber, peeled and cut lengthwise into 1/2-inch-wide strips
2 stalks celery, cut lengthwise into 1/2-inch-wide strips
1 cup extra-virgin olive oil
2 teaspoons Aceto Balsamico Tradizionale
Salt and freshly ground pepper to taste

Arrange the vegetables on a serving platter and place in the middle of the table.

Into each of 4 small serving dishes, pour 1/4 cup of the olive oil. Add 1/2 teaspoon of aceto balsamico, but do not stir.

Offer each guest a dipping dish, to season with salt and pepper to taste. *Serves 4*

Bread-Crumb Pasta in Broth

Passatelli in brodo is a quick soup and an innovative way to use leftover bread.
Be sure that the bread crumbs have been ground very fine. If you don't have a food mill,
you can pass the dough through the large holes of a grater. The result will be short,
stubby little "noodles," which will take 1 minute less to cook.

1 cup plus 3 tablespoons fine
dried bread crumbs
Salt and freshly ground pepper to taste
2 teaspoons finely grated orange zest
3 eggs
1 tablespoon Aceto Balsamico di Modena
1/3 cup grated Parmigiano-Reggiano
2 tablespoons unsalted butter,
at room temperature
6 cups rich chicken stock (page 106)

In a medium bowl, combine the bread crumbs, salt, pepper, and orange zest. Stir in the eggs and aceto balsamico, mixing well. Add the Parmigiano-Reggiano and butter, blending to form a smooth, but not sticky, dough.

In a large stockpot, bring the chicken stock to a boil. Pass the dough through the large holes of a food mill directly into the broth. Reduce to a simmer and cook for 3 to 4 minutes, or until pasta is cooked through but still slightly firm. Ladle into soup bowls and serve immediately.
Serves 4

Francescana's Cream of White Onion and Potato Soup

*After several months of working in New York, Massimo Bottura brought
a little piece of America back to Ristorante Francescana in Modena. On each table
in his charming restaurant are colorful plates, souvenirs from America.
The decor is artful, and the food is inspired.*

Capon Stock
1 gallon cold water
One 4-pound capon or chicken, cut into pieces
2 large carrots, peeled and cut into
1-inch pieces
1 large onion, cut into 1-inch pieces
2 stalks celery, cut into 1-inch pieces
1 sprig each fresh parsley and thyme
1 bay leaf

Soup
3 tablespoons extra-virgin olive oil,
plus more for garnish
4 medium white onions, chopped
8 scallions, chopped (white part only)
2 potatoes, peeled and chopped into
1/2-inch pieces
5 cups capon stock
Salt and freshly ground white pepper to taste
Aceto Balsamico Tradizionale to taste

To prepare the stock: Place all ingredients in a large nonreactive stockpot and bring to a boil.

Reduce temperature to a simmer and continue to cook, uncovered, for 3 hours. Skim impurities from the top occasionally.

Strain and discard the vegetables and capon pieces. Cool stock before refrigerating. After chilling, remove the fat layer. *Makes 3 quarts*

To make the soup: In a heavy pot over low heat, heat the 3 tablespoons olive oil. Add the onions and scallions and cook, stirring occasionally, for about 40 minutes. Do not brown.

In a covered pot, salt and steam the potatoes over boiling water for approximately 10 minutes, or until tender. Add the potatoes to the onions and slowly add the stock. Cook until heated through. In a blender or food processor, purée the mixture until smooth, in batches if necessary. Pass through a fine-meshed sieve. Add the salt and pepper.

Pour into warmed shallow soup dishes and finish with a drizzle of olive oil and aceto balsamico. *Serves 4*

Bite-Sized Polenta Squares

This recipe makes an impressive appetizer that can be made completely ahead.

2 tablespoons olive oil
1/4 cup finely chopped onion
1 clove garlic, minced
2 1/4 cups chicken stock (page 106)
3/4 cup polenta
1 tablespoon minced fresh parsley
1/2 teaspoon minced fresh thyme
Salt and freshly ground pepper to taste
2 ounces fresh white goat cheese, cut into
1/2-inch square pieces
1 tablespoon Aceto Balsamico Tradizionale

Lightly oil an 8-inch square baking dish. In a large saucepan over medium heat, heat the oil. Add the onion and sauté for 4 to 5 minutes, or until golden brown. Add the garlic and sauté until softened but not browned.

Add the chicken stock and bring to a boil. Gradually add the polenta to the stock, whisking constantly. Lower heat to medium and continue to cook, stirring constantly, for approximately 30 minutes, or until the polenta comes away from the side of the pot easily.

Stir in the parsley, thyme, salt, and pepper. Pour into the prepared dish, smoothing the top with a spatula. Set aside and let cool.

When ready to serve, cut the polenta into 1-inch squares. Top each square with a piece of goat cheese. With the end of a wooden spoon, make a small indentation in the goat cheese.

Transfer to a serving platter and place a drop of balsamico into the indentation in each piece of the goat cheese. Serve at room temperature.
Serves 6

Flatbreads Stuffed with Prosciutto and Arugula

Little trucks dot the roadsides of Emilia Romagna, offering commuters a surprising assortment of hot sandwiches made with fresh breads for a snack or quick lunch. One of my favorites is this piadina, *a griddled bread folded around a variety of toppings.*

2 cups unbleached all-purpose flour
1/2 teaspoon salt
1/2 teaspoon baking soda
3 tablespoons unsalted butter
1/2 cup warm water
1 teaspoon Aceto Balsamico di Modena
3 tablespoons extra-virgin olive oil, plus more for cooking
1 cup coarsely chopped arugula
Salt and freshly ground pepper to taste
8 thin slices prosciutto di Parma

In a large bowl, combine the flour, salt, and baking soda. Using a pastry cutter or 2 knives, cut in the butter, distributing it throughout the dough until the mixture resembles coarse crumbs. Using a fork, stir in just enough water to moisten the dry mixture. Form the dough into a ball. On a lightly floured surface, knead the dough until it is smooth and not sticky. Divide the dough into 8 equal pieces.

Roll the dough out into 6-inch rounds about 1/8 inch thick.

In a small bowl, whisk the aceto balsamico into the olive oil. Add the arugula, tossing to coat well. Season with salt and pepper. Set aside.

Heat a large, heavy skillet over medium-high heat, and coat it lightly with olive oil. Cook the dough rounds for about 1 minute on each side, or until lightly browned.

While still warm, top each bread with 2 slices prosciutto and a pinch of the dressed arugula. Fold in half and eat immediately. *Serves 4*

"CALLING ACETO
BALSAMICO VINEGAR
IS LIKE CALLING
PAVAROTTI
A STREET SINGER."

—FRED PLOTKIN,
*ITALY FOR THE
GOURMET TRAVELER*

Chicken Liver Crostini

This classic appetizer is often made with lemon juice and lemon zest.
Using balsamic vinegar instead adds a pleasant sweetness.

1 tablespoon unsalted butter
2 tablespoons olive oil
2 tablespoons finely chopped
pancetta (³/4 ounce)
¹/2 onion, finely chopped
6 ounces chicken livers
¹/4 cup dry white wine
2 tablespoons Aceto Balsamico di Modena
¹/2 teaspoon minced fresh thyme leaves
1 tablespoon minced fresh flat-leaf parsley, plus
12 leaves for garnish
Salt and freshly ground pepper to taste
12 slices bread, toasted
1 unpeeled Red Delicious apple, cored and
cut into thin slices

In a large sauté pan or skillet, melt the butter with the olive oil over medium heat. Add the pancetta and onion and sauté for 4 to 5 minutes, or until the onion is golden brown. Add the chicken livers and white wine; cook for 12 to 15 minutes, or until the livers turn just slightly pink at the center. Add the aceto balsamico and stir to loosen cooked bits from the bottom of the pan. Transfer the mixture to a blender or food processor and purée. Return to the pan and add the thyme, minced parsley, salt, and pepper. Bring to a simmer and cook for 5 minutes more. Remove from the heat and let cool.

Just before serving, spread the chicken liver mixture on the toasted bread. Place 1 leaf of parsley and 1 slice of apple on each toast. *Serves 6*

Zanasi's Radicchio Salad with Parmigiano-Reggiano and Aceto Balsamico

Valeriano Zanasi and his wife, Orianna Cuoghi, maintain a pristine acetaia in their home to make aceto balsamico for their own use and for gifts. This salad illustrates the fact that with outstanding ingredients, the simplest preparation is the best.

Leaves from 2 heads radicchio
Salt to taste
3 teaspoons Aceto Balsamico Tradizionale or
to taste
1/3 cup extra-virgin olive oil or to taste
4 ounces Parmigiano-Reggiano, thinly shaved with
a truffle or cheese slicer

Place the radicchio leaves in a salad bowl. Sprinkle salt over the leaves, add 1 1/2 teaspoons of the aceto balsamico, and toss well. Drizzle liberally with the olive oil and toss lightly. Sprinkle the Parmigiano-Reggiano over the salad. Drizzle the remaining 1 1/2 teaspoons aceto balsamico over the cheese. Serve immediately. *Serves 4*

Foie Gras with Mostarda di Cremona

Cremona, in the northern region of Lombardy, is famous for mostarda, *a mixture of candied fruits preserved in a blend of sugar and mustard-flavored oil. It can be found in gourmet Italian food stores packed in jars or beautifully decorated tins. If you are unable to find* mostarda, *try substituting your favorite mango chutney.*

12 ounces fresh foie gras, chilled
Flour for dredging
Salt and freshly ground pepper to taste
1 tablespoon extra-virgin olive oil
1/4 cup Aceto Balsamico di Modena
1 cup veal stock (page 107)
1/4 cup coarsely chopped
mostarda di Cremona

Slice the foie gras into 1/2-inch thick slices. Place the flour in a shallow dish and season with salt and pepper. Lightly dust both sides of the foie gras with the flour.

Heat a medium sauté pan or skillet over high heat and coat with the oil. Sauté the foie gras until lightly browned, about 30 seconds per side. Transfer to paper towels to drain. Set aside and keep warm.

Return the pan to medium heat, add the balsamico, and stir to loosen any cooked particles from the bottom of the pan. Add the stock and cook to reduce by half. Season with salt and pepper to taste.

Divide the sauce equally among 4 serving dishes. Place the warm foie gras on top and garnish each serving with 1 tablespoon of the *mostarda. Serves 4*

Tuscan Bread Salad

*Panzanella is a salad designed to use leftover bread, typically made
with red wine vinegar. This version uses aceto balsamico. If using fresh bread,
lightly toast it before cutting into cubes. As this salad stands, the bread
absorbs the dressing. Be sure to serve it at room temperature.*

3 cups 1/2-inch cubes day-old Italian bread
2 ripe tomatoes, seeded, cut into
1/2-inch pieces
1 cucumber, peeled, seeded, and chopped into
1/2-inch chunks
1/2 cup chopped green bell pepper
1/2 cup finely chopped red onion
3 cloves garlic, minced
1/4 cup Aceto Balsamico di Modena
1 cup fresh basil leaves, plus
3 sprigs fresh basil for garnish
1/3 cup olive oil
Salt and freshly ground pepper to taste

In a mixing bowl, combine the bread cubes, tomatoes, cucumber, bell pepper, and red onion.

In a blender or food processor, purée the garlic, balsamico, and basil until smooth. With the machine running, slowly drizzle in the olive oil. Season with salt and pepper.

Toss the bread and vegetable mixture with the dressing, garnish with basil sprigs, and serve immediately. *Serves 6*

Roasted Asparagus

Other seasonal vegetables can be substituted for this quick and easy starter.
For example, try baby zucchini, carrot rounds, or broccoli florets. Adjust the blanching time
according to the size of the vegetable, taking care not to overcook.

1 pound asparagus spears, trimmed
1/4 cup extra-virgin olive oil
1 tablespoon Aceto Balsamico Tradizionale
Salt and freshly ground pepper to taste

Preheat the oven to 400°. Lightly oil a baking sheet.

Blanch the asparagus in boiling salted water for 30 seconds. Immerse them immediately in ice water to stop the cooking. Drain and place on the prepared pan.

Drizzle the asparagus with olive oil and roast in the oven for 12 to 15 minutes, or until tender and lightly browned.

Arrange the asparagus on a serving platter and drizzle with the aceto balsamico and season to taste with salt and pepper. *Serves 6*

"ACETO BALSAMICO
IS BORN OF SUGAR,
NOT ALCOHOL."

—RENATO
BERGONZINI,
MODENA

Side
Dishes

Polenta Laced with Pancetta and Ruby Chard

This polenta is substantial enough to serve as a main dish at lunch.
With a salad and some fresh bread, it is a satisfying and complete meal.

2 tablespoons olive oil
1/2 cup chopped onion
2 ounces pancetta, chopped
2 cloves garlic, minced
1 pound red chard (leaves only), cut into julienne
4 1/2 cups chicken stock (page 106)
1 1/2 cups polenta
Salt and freshly ground pepper to taste
1/4 cup freshly grated Parmigiano-Reggiano
2 tablespoons minced fresh flat-leaf parsley
1 tablespoon Aceto Balsamico Tradizionale

In a large sauté pan or skillet over medium heat, heat the oil and cook the onion and pancetta until the onion is golden brown, 4 to 5 minutes. Add the garlic and cook until softened but not browned. Add the chard and cook until any liquid has evaporated. Set aside and let cool.

In a large, heavy saucepan, bring the chicken stock to a boil. Gradually add the polenta, whisking constantly. Lower heat to medium and continue to cook, stirring constantly for about 30 minutes, or until the polenta comes away from the side of the pot easily.

Stir the chard mixture into the polenta. Season with salt and pepper to taste. Transfer to a warmed serving dish. Sprinkle with the Parmigiano-Reggiano, minced parsley, and aceto balsamico. Serve immediately. *Serves 8*

Eggplant Rollatini

You can also serve these rollatini without the tomato dressing as an appetizer passed on a tray at parties—great finger food!

1 large eggplant, peeled and
cut lengthwise into ¹/₄-inch-thick slices
Sea salt for sprinkling
Extra-virgin olive oil for brushing, plus
3 tablespoons olive oil
1 cup ricotta cheese
2 cloves garlic, minced
1 tablespoon minced fresh basil, plus
1 tablespoon julienned fresh basil
2 tablespoons Aceto Balsamico Tradizionale
Salt and freshly ground pepper to taste
1 large tomato, peeled, seeded, and
diced (see page 107)

Light a fire in a charcoal grill or preheat a gas grill or broiler.

Sprinkle the eggplant with salt on both sides and let drain for 30 minutes on a wire rack. Rinse off the salt and pat dry with paper towels. Brush lightly with olive oil. Grill or broil the eggplant on both sides until lightly browned.

Set aside to cool.

In a small bowl, blend the ricotta cheese, garlic, minced basil, and 1 tablespoon of the aceto balsamico together; season with salt and pepper. Refrigerate for at least 1 hour.

Spread a thin layer of the cheese mixture on each piece of eggplant. Roll each piece lengthwise into a tight roll. Place seam-side down on a tray and refrigerate for 1 hour.

To serve, cut crosswise into 1-inch-thick slices and arrange on a platter. Let warm to room temperature. Combine the tomato, 3 tablespoons olive oil, julienned basil, and remaining 1 tablespoon of the aceto balsamico. Season with salt and pepper to taste and spoon over the eggplant. *Serves 4*

"BETWEEN WINE
AND GRAPE THERE
IS A DIRECT
RELATIONSHIP.
BETWEEN VINEGAR
AND GRAPE
IS MAN'S
INTERVENTION."

—FERDINANDO
CAVALLI,
SCANDIANO

Villa Gaidello's Aceto Balsamico-Marinated Cipolline

*Paola Bini runs a simply wonderful inn and restaurant
in Castelfranco Emilia. She makes extraordinary homemade preserves there,
like these small flat onions preserved in balsamic vinegar.*

4 cups white wine vinegar
3¹/2 tablespoons granulated sugar
A pinch of coarse salt
*2 pounds cipolline onions, about 1¹/2 inches
in diameter, trimmed and peeled*
4 cups Aceto Balsamico di Modena
3¹/2 tablespoons packed light brown sugar

In a large nonreactive pot, combine the wine vinegar, granulated sugar, and salt. Bring to a boil, add the onions, and cook for 2 to 3 minutes.

In a medium nonreactive saucepan, combine the aceto balsamico and brown sugar. Heat over medium heat until the sugar is dissolved; do not boil.

Drain the onions and divide them among 5 hot, sterilized pint jars. Add the hot aceto balsamico mixture, covering the onions. Seal the jars and refrigerate for up to 1 month, or process in a hot-water bath according to the manufacturer's instructions. *Makes 5 pints*

Peperonata

*The flavor of this dish actually improves when it ages for a day or two. As it stands,
the flavors marry, and when it is reheated, the fusion is enhanced.*

2 large sweet onions, sliced
5 tablespoons unsalted butter
5 tablespoons extra-virgin olive oil
1 each yellow, red, and green bell pepper,
seeded, deribbed, and cut into strips
5 Roma tomatoes, peeled, seeded, and
coarsely chopped (see page 107)
1 tablespoon Aceto Balsamico di Modena
Salt to taste
1 tablespoon water

Put the onions in a large saucepan, and cook over medium heat until the moisture is released and evaporated, about 3 to 4 minutes. Add the butter and olive oil and cook for 6 to 8 minutes, or until the onions are golden brown. Add the peppers and tomatoes. Cook for 4 to 5 minutes, or until the water from the vegetables is evaporated. Add the aceto balsamico and salt. Cook for 3 to 4 minutes, or until the aceto balsamico is absorbed. Add the water, cover, and cook for 5 minutes, or until completely heated through.
Serves 4

Fresh Fava Beans Simmered in Aceto Balsamico Broth

*Peeling the larger fava beans, but leaving the skins on some of the smaller beans
adds more color and texture to this dish.*

2 pounds fresh fava beans, shelled
3 tablespoons olive oil
1 onion, diced
1 small carrot, peeled and finely chopped
1 stalk celery, finely chopped
3 tablespoons Aceto Balsamico di Modena
2 cups rich chicken stock (page 106)
Salt and freshly ground pepper to taste

Blanch the fava beans in boiling salted water for 1 minute, then immerse immediately in ice water. Peel two-thirds of the beans by pinching the end of each bean and squeezing it out of the skin. Leave about one-third of the smallest beans unskinned.

In a large saucepan over medium heat, heat the oil and sauté the onion, carrot, and celery for 4 to 5 minutes, or until golden brown. Add the aceto balsamico, and stir to loosen cooked bits from the bottom of the pan. Add the stock and bring to a boil.

Add the fava beans and decrease heat to a simmer. Cook for 5 to 7 minutes, or until the fava beans are completely warmed through. Season with salt and pepper. *Serves 4*

Four Seasons Frittata

Vegetables representing each season embellish this beautiful egg dish: sweet red pepper for summer, mushrooms for fall, asparagus for spring, and potato for winter.

6 eggs, lightly beaten
1 tablespoon minced fresh flat-leaf parsley
Salt and freshly ground pepper to taste
3 tablespoons olive oil
1 small onion, diced
5 ounces mushrooms, sliced
1 red bell pepper, seeded, deribbed, and sliced 1/4 inch thick
8 ounces asparagus tips, blanched
1 potato, peeled, halved, cut into 1/4 inch thick crosswise slices, and blanched
1/4 cup freshly grated Parmigiano-Reggiano
2 teaspoons Aceto Balsamico Tradizionale

Preheat the oven to 425°.

In a small bowl, lightly beat the eggs. Add the parsley and season with salt and pepper to taste. Set aside.

In a medium ovenproof sauté pan or skillet, heat the oil and sauté the onion until lightly browned, 4 to 5 minutes. Add the mushrooms and cook until they are softened and the liquid has evaporated. Remove with a slotted spoon and set aside.

Pour the egg mixture into the hot pan and cook over medium heat for 3 to 4 minutes, or until it just begins to set.

Arrange each kind of vegetable in one of 4 quadrants on top of the eggs. Sprinkle the Parmigiano-Reggiano on top and bake for 10 to 15 minutes, or until a knife inserted in the center comes out clean. Drizzle with the aceto balsamico. Serve immediately or let cool to room temperature. *Serves 4*

EVERY TRADITIONAL
BALSAMIC VINEGAR
STARTS WITH THE
SAME ESSENTIALS:
GRAPES, BARRELS,
AND TIME-HONORED
TRADITIONS.

Pasta

Raviolo of Mixed Summer Vegetables

This single large raviolo makes a colorful and elegant first course.

Filling and Sauce
1/4 cup plus 3 tablespoons extra-virgin olive oil
1/2 red onion, finely diced
1 red bell pepper, seeded, deribbed, and finely diced
1 zucchini, finely diced
1 cup fresh corn kernels
Salt and freshly ground pepper to taste
1 tablespoon minced fresh basil
1/2 cup ricotta cheese
1 teaspoon finely grated lemon zest

1 tablespoon fresh lemon juice
1 tablespoon Aceto Balsamico Tradizionale

Pasta Dough
1 pound fresh pasta dough, last roll out
not completed (page 105)
1 cup fresh flat-leaf parsley leaves

1 egg beaten with 1 teaspoon water
1 tablespoon extra-virgin olive oil
1 tablespoon Aceto Balsamico Tradizionale

To make the filling and sauce: In a medium sauté pan or skillet over medium heat, heat the 1/4 cup olive oil and sauté the onion and red pepper 3 to 4 minutes, or until softened but not browned. Add the zucchini and corn and sauté for 3 to 4 minutes longer, or until softened. Season with salt and pepper; remove from heat and let cool.

Divide the vegetables between two bowls. Stir the basil, ricotta, lemon zest, and lemon juice into one bowl. In the other bowl, add the 3 tablespoons olive oil and aceto balsamico. Set aside.

To make the pasta: Follow the instructions for making pasta dough. When you are ready to roll the dough for the last time, arrange the parsley leaves randomly in a single layer on half of the dough. Fold in half and pass through the pasta maker one more time. Cut into twelve 5-inch squares, taking care not to cut through a parsley leaf. Set aside.

To assemble, place 2 heaping tablespoons vegetable-ricotta mixture on 6 of the pasta squares. Brush the edges with the egg mixture and top with another pasta square, pressing the edges firmly together to seal, taking care that the filling doesn't break the seal.

Drop the ravioli into a large pot of salted briskly boiling water. Cook for 2 to 3 minutes, or until the ravioli are al dente.

Drain and place on individual serving plates. With a very sharp knife, make a slit in the top to expose the filling. Sprinkle the vegetable-balsamico mixture around each raviolo and drizzle the top with the olive oil and aceto balsamico. Serve immediately. *Serves 6*

Pansotti with Gorgonzola Dolcelatte, Walnuts, and Aceto Balsamico

The dolcelatte, or sweet milk, style of Gorgonzola is a creamier, younger version of this cheese, delicious as a filling for ravioli. If you use regular Gorgonzola, bear in mind that it is much stronger; blend it with a little ricotta if you want a milder flavor.

6 ounces Gorgonzola dolcelatte, at room temperature
2 tablespoons heavy cream
1/2 cup walnuts, toasted and chopped (see page 107)
1 teaspoon minced fresh thyme
Pasta Dough, unrolled (page 105)
1 egg beaten with 1 teaspoon water
Extra-virgin olive oil and Aceto Balsamico Tradizionale for drizzling

In a small bowl, combine the Gorgonzola and cream, beating until smooth. Fold in 1/4 cup of the walnuts and the thyme; mix well.

Roll out the pasta dough and cut into 3-inch squares. Cut each square in half diagonally to form 2 triangles. Place a teaspoonful of the Gorgonzola mixture in the center of each triangle. Brush the edges with the egg mixture and fold the triangle in half. Press the edges firmly to seal the triangle. Repeat to fill the remaining triangles.

Cook in salted gently boiling water for 3 to 4 minutes, or until al dente. Drain and drizzle with olive oil and aceto balsamico to taste. Sprinkle with the remaining 1/4 cup walnuts and serve immediately. *Serves 6*

Tagliatelle with Duck Ragù

The sauce can be made ahead and reheated to toss with the pasta just before serving.

3 tablespoons extra-virgin olive oil
2 large onions, diced
2 carrots, peeled and diced
1 stalk celery, diced
1 duck (about 3 pounds), skinned, deboned, and
coarsely ground
1/4 cup Aceto Balsamico di Modena
4 large tomatoes, peeled, seeded, and
coarsely chopped (see page 107)
1 tablespoon minced fresh flat-leaf parsley
1 teaspoon minced fresh rosemary
1/2 teaspoon minced fresh thyme
Salt and freshly ground pepper to taste
1 1/2 pounds fresh tagliatelle pasta

In a large sauté pan or skillet over medium heat, heat the olive oil and cook the onions, carrots, and celery for 3 to 4 minutes, or until softened. Add the ground duck and cook, stirring, for 4 to 5 minutes, or until browned.

Add the aceto balsamico and stir to scrape up cooked bits from the bottom of the pan. Add the tomatoes, parsley, rosemary, and thyme. Reduce heat to a simmer and cook, uncovered, for 20 to 30 minutes, or until thickened. Season with salt and pepper to taste. Set the ragù aside and keep warm.

In a large pot of salted boiling water, cook the pasta until al dente. Drain and toss with the sauce. Serve immediately. *Serves 6*

Tortellini in Brodo

*Stories abound detailing the origin of this famous pasta. My favorite is
the one about the innkeeper/chef who was inspired to invent the dish after peering
through a keyhole at a beautiful woman bathing. The sight of her navel in the bathwater
led to the creation of the dish we know as tortellini bathing in a vessel of rich broth.*

2 ounces prosciutto di Parma
4 ounces ground veal loin
3/4 cup freshly grated Parmigiano-Reggiano
2 tablespoons Aceto Balsamico di Modena
Pasta Dough (page 105)
1 egg beaten with 1 teaspoon water
10 cups rich chicken stock (page 106)
2 tablespoons finely shredded fresh basil

In a food processor, grind the prosciutto. Transfer to a bowl and stir in the ground veal, $1/2$ cup of the Parmigiano-Reggiano, and the aceto balsamico. Place in a piping bag and set aside.

Cut the pasta into 2-inch rounds. Pipe about $1/2$ teaspoon prosciutto mixture in the center of each round, brush the edges with the egg mixture, and fold in half to form a half-moon shape. Wrap it around your finger, bringing the corners together to overlap, and pinch tightly to seal the shape into a circle. Curl the thin edges of the pasta back. Set aside on a lightly floured surface to air-dry until the stock is ready.

In a large pot, bring the chicken stock to a boil. Add the tortellini and cook for 3 to 5 minutes, or until al dente. Ladle into warmed serving dishes and sprinkle with basil and the remaining $1/4$ cup Parmigiano-Reggiano. *Serves 6*

Pumpkin Gnocchi in Aceto Balsamico Cream Sauce

The Italian pumpkin is quite sweet and moist. Standard American pumpkins
are not as sweet; an excellent substitute is butternut squash.

8 ounces pumpkin, halved and seeded
1 baking potato, baked and cooled
2 1/2 cups unbleached all-purpose flour, plus
flour for dusting
1 teaspoon salt

1 egg, beaten
2 cups heavy cream
1 cup rich chicken stock (page 106)
1/4 cup Aceto Balsamico di Modena

Preheat the oven to 375°. Line a baking sheet with parchment paper.

Place the pumpkin cut-side down on the prepared pan and bake for 25 to 30 minutes, or until soft and lightly browned. Let cool, scoop out the flesh, and put it through a ricer or food mill into a bowl. Scoop out the baked potato flesh and put it through a ricer or food mill into the same bowl with the pumpkin.

In a large bowl, combine the 2 1/2 cups flour and the salt. Make a well in the center of the flour and add the pumpkin-potato mixture and egg. Work into the flour by hand until the mixture can be formed into a ball.

On a lightly floured surface, knead the mixture for 5 to 8 minutes, or until soft and smooth.

Divide the dough into 4 pieces, and using the palms of your hands, roll each piece into a sausage shape about 1/2 inch in diameter. Cut into 1-inch lengths. Dust lightly with flour and press against the tines of a fork while making a small indentation with your finger on the other side. Set aside on a lightly floured surface until ready to cook.

In a medium saucepan, combine the cream, chicken stock, and aceto balsamico. Simmer over medium heat for 4 to 5 minutes, or until completely heated through.

In a large pot of salted boiling water, cook the gnocchi for 3 to 5 minutes, or until tender but still slightly firm. Drain, toss with the cream sauce, and serve immediately. *Serves 6*

Spaghetti with Grilled Vegetables Marinated in Aceto Balsamico

This is the perfect summer meal, served with a fresh green salad and a crisp white wine. The vegetables can also be grilled and marinated ahead, making it a quick weeknight dinner.

*1/2 cup extra-virgin olive oil, plus
oil for brushing
2 shallots, minced
1/4 cup Aceto Balsamico di Modena
2 Japanese eggplants, cut into
1/2-inch-thick lengthwise slices
6 baby zucchini, trimmed*

*1 red bell pepper, seeded, deveined, and
cut into eighths
4 shiitake mushrooms, stemmed and halved
12 tiny new potatoes, halved and
cooked until tender
Salt and freshly ground pepper to taste
1 pound spaghetti*

Light a fire in a charcoal grill or preheat a gas grill.

In a medium saucepan over medium-high heat, heat the 1/2 cup olive oil. Add the shallots and cook until softened but not browned. Stir in the aceto balsamico and remove from heat.

Brush the eggplants, zucchini, pepper, mushrooms, and potatoes with olive oil. Season with salt and pepper. Grill over medium-high heat for 3 to 4 minutes on each side, or until lightly browned.

Place the vegetables in a shallow nonreactive dish and pour the aceto balsamico mixture over. Let stand for 30 minutes at room temperature, or overnight in the refrigerator.

To serve, if using refrigerated vegetables, let them warm to room temperature. In a large pot of salted boiling water, cook the spaghetti until al dente. Drain. Toss with the vegetables and serve immediately. *Serves 6*

Maltagliati e Fagioli/Pasta and Beans

Maltagliati *literally means "poorly cut." To make it, a fresh sheet
of pasta is rolled and cut into random shapes. It is also a great way to use the scraps
of dough left over from making other pasta shapes and noodles.*

1 cup dried borlotti (cranberry) beans
3 cloves garlic
3 fresh sage leaves
3 tablespoons olive oil
1 onion, finely chopped
1 carrot, peeled and finely chopped
1 stalk celery, finely chopped
6 to 7 cups chicken stock (page 106)
1 tablespoon minced fresh flat-leaf parsley
1 teaspoon minced fresh thyme
Pasta Dough (page 105)
1/4 cup Aceto Balsamico di Modena
Salt and freshly ground pepper to taste

Soak the beans overnight in water to cover with the garlic and sage.

The next day, drain the beans, reserving the garlic and sage. In a large saucepan over medium heat, heat the 3 tablespoons oil and sauté the onion, carrot, and celery until golden brown, 6 to 8 minutes. Add 6 cups chicken stock, drained beans, garlic, and sage. Bring to a boil, then decrease to a simmer. Add the parsley and thyme and cook, uncovered, for 2 to 2 1/2 hours, or until the beans are tender.

With a sharp knife, cut the fresh pasta into irregular shapes. Add the pasta to the beans and cook until al dente, 4 to 6 minutes. Stir in the aceto balsamico. The dish will be thick; add a little chicken stock to thin if necessary. Season with salt and pepper. *Serves 6 to 8*

Risotto with Roasted Chicken and Fennel

This dark, rich risotto is an excellent way to use leftover roasted chicken.
(Use the bones to make the stock.) If you are roasting the chicken just for this recipe,
roast the fennel and onion with the chicken for the last 15 minutes, adding them
to the risotto at the end with the chicken.

1/4 cup extra-virgin olive oil
1 onion, diced
1 bulb fennel, trimmed and julienned, some fronds reserved for garnish
1 1/2 cups Carnaroli or Arborio rice
1/4 cup Aceto Balsamico di Modena
7 1/2 to 8 cups roasted chicken stock (page 106), heated
2 cups cubed roasted chicken meat
2 tablespoons unsalted butter
Salt and freshly ground pepper to taste

In a medium saucepan over medium heat, heat the olive oil and sauté the onion and fennel until softened but not browned, about 3 minutes. Add the rice and stir until it is opaque, 3 to 4 minutes. Add the aceto balsamico and stir until the vinegar is absorbed.

Add 1 cup stock to the rice, and constantly stir until most of the liquid is absorbed. Repeat until all but 1/4 cup of the stock is used and the rice is al dente. This should take 18 to 20 minutes.

Add the remaining stock and the chicken, and stir in the butter. Season with salt and pepper, garnish with reserved fennel fronds, and serve immediately. *Serves 6*

Main
Dishes

Stinco di Maiale / Pork Shanks

Stinco is typically made with veal shanks, but pork is a nice variation.
Serve on a bed of pasta, such as pappardelle.

2 pork shanks (2 pounds each), cut by
butcher into ¹/2-inch slices
Salt and freshly ground pepper to taste
¹/4 cup olive oil
1 large onion, sliced
¹/2 cup Aceto Balsamico di Modena
1 carrot, peeled and diced
1 stalk celery, diced
2 boiling potatoes, peeled and diced
3 cups beef or veal stock (page 107)
2 tablespoons Aceto Balsamico Tradizionale
3 tablespoons minced fresh flat-leaf parsley

Preheat the oven to 450°. Season the pork shanks with salt and pepper.

In a large, heavy roasting pan over medium heat, heat the olive oil and brown the pork shanks on all sides. Add the onion. Place in the oven and roast for 30 minutes.

Remove the pan from the oven and add the Aceto Balsamico di Modena. Add the carrot, celery, potatoes, and stock and return pan to the oven for 45 minutes, or until the meat is very tender. Transfer the meat and vegetables to a serving casserole and keep warm.

Pour the pan juices into a saucepan and cook over high heat until reduced by half. Return the vegetables to the sauce and heat through. Add the Aceto Balsamico Tradizionale, season with salt and pepper to taste, and spoon the sauce over the shanks. Sprinkle with the minced parsley and serve immediately. *Serves 6*

Pork Roasted with Apples, Honey, and Aceto Balsamico

This dish, which is wonderful during the holidays, is best served with sautéed greens.

One 4-pound boneless pork loin roast
Salt and freshly ground pepper to taste
3 tablespoons extra-virgin olive oil
2 cups beef or veal stock (page 107)
3 tablespoons honey
3 tablespoons Aceto Balsamico di Modena
3 pounds Yellow Finn potatoes, peeled and quartered

3 Granny Smith or Pippin apples,
peeled, cored, and diced
4 cloves garlic
1 teaspoon minced fresh thyme
1 tablespoon cornstarch mixed with
2 tablespoons water
2 tablespoons Aceto Balsamico Tradizionale

Preheat the oven to 375°. Season the pork with salt and pepper.

In a heavy, heatproof casserole or Dutch oven over medium heat, heat the oil and brown the pork on all sides.

Meanwhile, combine the stock, honey, and the Aceto Balsamico di Modena in a medium saucepan. Cook over medium heat until the honey has dissolved and the mixture is well blended. Pour the hot liquid into the pan with the pork. Cover the pan, transfer it to the oven, and bake for 2 hours.

Add the potatoes and bake for 15 minutes.

Add the apples, garlic, and thyme and bake for 15 to 20 minutes, or until the potatoes are tender and the pork registers 185° in the center.

Transfer the pork to a serving platter. Set aside and keep warm. Strain the cooking liquid into a saucepan. Bring to a boil and decrease heat to medium. Whisk the cornstarch mixture into the cooking juices and cook, stirring constantly, until slightly thickened. Season with salt and pepper. With a slotted spoon, arrange the potatoes and apples around the roast. Drizzle the roast, potatoes, and apples with Aceto Balsamico Tradizionale. Serve the sauce on the side. *Serves 6*

Cold Fillet of Beef with Warm Balsamic Dressing

This dressing can also be refrigerated and served chilled.
Blend it well before dressing the dish.

One 2-pound beef tenderloin
Salt and freshly ground pepper to taste
3 tablespoons extra-virgin olive oil
3 ounces pancetta, chopped
2 shallots, peeled and minced
1/4 cup Aceto Balsamico di Modena
1 1/2 cups veal or beef stock (page 107)
6 cups baby spinach leaves

Season the beef liberally with salt and pepper. In a large sauté pan or skillet over medium-high heat, heat the olive oil and brown the tenderloin on all sides. Transfer to a cutting board and let cool.

Add the pancetta to the pan. Cook over medium heat for 4 to 5 minutes, or until golden brown. Add the shallots and cook until softened, about 2 minutes. Add the aceto balsamico, stirring to loosen the cooked bits from the bottom of the pan. Add the veal stock and cook over high heat until reduced by half.

Slice the cooled steak very thin (the meat will be rare). Divide the spinach leaves evenly among the plates. Arrange the sliced beef in a fan on top of the spinach. Spoon the warm sauce over the meat and spinach. Season with salt and pepper to taste. Serve immediately. *Serves 6*

Otello's Fillets of Veal

Otello Bonfatti works with the Barbieri family at Acetaia del Cristo in the San Prospero community on the outskirts of Modena. This is his version of a classic dish found on almost every local restaurant menu. In restaurants, however, it is served with Aceto Balsamico di Modena whereas Otello uses only traditional balsamic vinegar, and plenty of it!

2 scallops of veal, about 4 ounces each
1 clove garlic
Flour for dredging
2 tablespoons extra-virgin olive oil
1 stalk celery, diced
Salt and freshly ground pepper to taste
4 teaspoons Aceto Balsamico Tradizionale

Using the flat side of a meat mallet or a rolling pin, pound the veal to an even thickness of $1/2$ inch. Cut the garlic in half and rub the cut sides on both sides of the meat.

Dredge the veal in the flour, coating both sides. Shake off the excess flour.

In a large sauté pan or skillet over medium heat, heat the olive oil and cook the celery until softened, 3 to 4 minutes. Push the celery aside, add the veal, and cook for 1 minute on each side. Season with salt and pepper. Remove the pan from the heat and pour 2 teaspoons of aceto balsamico over each piece of veal. Serve immediately. *Serves 2*

Maura's Aceto Balsamico—Marinated Rabbit

Maura Benatti is the wife of Francesco Renzi, Modena's master cooper.
From their personal acetaia *they make aceto balsamico only for their own family*
and for very dear friends. Maura uses balsamic vinegar as a marinade
for rabbit, giving it a succulent tenderness.

1/4 cup Aceto Balsamico di Modena
1/4 cup plus 3 tablespoons extra-virgin olive oil
2 cloves garlic, crushed
1 teaspoon juniper berries
1 bay leaf
1 stem fresh rosemary
Salt and freshly ground pepper to taste
One rabbit (about 21/3 pounds), cut into 8 pieces

In a large nonreactive casserole, combine the aceto balsamico, the 1/4 cup olive oil, the garlic, juniper berries, bay leaf, rosemary, salt, and pepper. Toss with the rabbit to coat well. Cover and refrigerate for at least 8 hours or overnight. Turn the pieces occasionally to ensure contact with the marinade.

Drain the rabbit, reserving the marinade, and let stand at room temperature for about 20 minutes. In a large sauté pan or skillet over medium heat, heat the 3 tablespoons olive oil. Add the rabbit pieces and cook until golden brown, 5 to 7 minutes. Gradually add the marinade to the pan, stirring to loosen the cooked bits from the bottom of the pan. Reduce heat to a simmer, cover, and cook for 20 minutes, or until the rabbit is very tender. Transfer the rabbit to a serving platter and keep warm. Cook the pan juices uncovered over high heat to reduce the liquid until slightly thickened. Season with salt and pepper. Transfer to a serving platter and serve immediately. *Serves 4*

Seared Loin of Lamb with Almond-Mint Pesto and Aceto Balsamico Glaze

*These lamb medallions are also delicious garnished with whole heads
of roasted garlic (page 107). The Almond-Mint Pesto can be made ahead; just cover
it with a thin layer of olive oil, seal in an airtight container, and refrigerate.*

Almond-Mint Pesto
3 cloves garlic
*1 bunch fresh mint, stemmed (about 1 cup tightly
packed leaves)*
1/2 cup almonds, toasted (see page 107)
Juice of 1 lemon
*3 tablespoons extra-virgin olive oil, or
to desired consistency*

2 pounds lamb tenderloin
Salt and freshly ground pepper to taste
5 tablespoons unsalted butter
3 tablespoons Aceto Balsamico di Modena
1 cup veal stock (page 107)
3 tablespoons minced fresh flat-leaf parsley

To make the pesto: In a food processor or blender, purée the garlic. Add the mint, almonds, and lemon juice, and process to a grainy texture. With the machine running, gradually add olive oil to the desired consistency. Set aside.

Tie the lamb loin with kitchen string at 1-inch intervals to maintain its shape. Liberally salt and pepper all sides. In a large skillet, melt 3 tablespoons of the butter over medium heat and cook until golden brown. Add the lamb loin and cook until lightly browned on all sides, about 4 minutes. Transfer to a cutting board and let cool.

Add the aceto balsamico to the pan, stirring to loosen cooked bits from the bottom of the pan. Add the veal stock and cook until reduced by half. Whisk in the remaining butter and season with salt and pepper to taste.

Cutting midway between the string ties, slice the lamb loin into 1-inch thick medallions. Arrange the medallions on an ovenproof platter. Spoon the sauce over the lamb and place in a warm oven for no more than 10 minutes.

Sprinkle with parsley and serve immediately, with the mint pesto on the side. *Serves 6*

Breast of Turkey with Grape-Balsamic Chutney

Use this chutney as a condiment on other meats, such as grilled chicken, or roasted sea bass.

Grape-Balsamic Chutney
1/2 cup Aceto Balsamico di Modena
1/2 cup granulated sugar
1/4 cup packed light brown sugar
1 1/2 pounds grapes, halved and seeded if necessary
1 small onion, finely chopped
2 cloves garlic, minced
1 yellow bell pepper, seeded, deribbed, and diced
2 teaspoons grated orange zest

2 pounds skinless, boneless turkey breast, cut into
1-inch-thick slices
Salt and freshly ground pepper to taste
2 cups cooked rice
4 teaspoons minced fresh thyme plus
8 sprigs for garnish
2 tablespoons minced fresh flat-leaf parsley
6 tablespoons extra-virgin olive oil
4 leeks, white part only, julienned
4 cups chicken stock (page 106)

To prepare the chutney: In a heavy, nonreactive pot, combine the aceto balsamico and sugars. Bring to a boil, stirring often, then add the remaining ingredients, mixing thoroughly. Return to a boil, then decrease heat to a simmer and cook for 5 minutes, or until completely heated through. Do not overcook the fruit. Let cool. (If not using soon, the chutney can be stored in sterilized glass jars in the refrigerator for up to 4 weeks.) *Makes 3 half-pints*

Preheat the oven to 375°. Lightly oil a 13 x 9-inch baking dish.

Using the flat side of a meat mallet or a rolling pin, pound the turkey slices between 2 sheets of plastic wrap to an even thickness of 1/4 inch. Sprinkle one side with salt and pepper. Spoon about 1 tablespoon of the rice down the middle of each slice. Sprinkle with the thyme and parsley and roll into a cylinder. Tie with kitchen string in several places to secure the cylinder shape.

In a large sauté pan or skillet, over medium heat, heat the oil and lightly brown the turkey rolls on all sides, a total of about 4 minutes. Transfer the rolls to the prepared dish and set aside. In the same sauté pan or skillet, sauté the leeks for 3 to 4 minutes, or until softened. Add the chicken stock, stirring to loosen all cooked bits from the bottom of the pan. Pour the mixture over the turkey rolls and bake them for 10 to 12 minutes, or until completely heated through.

Garnish with thyme sprigs and serve the Grape-Balsamic Chutney on the side. *Serves 8*

Breast of Duck with Onion-Balsamic Marmalade

*Sweet onions make the best marmalade; Vidalia, Maui, and Walla Walla
are three good varieties. A delicious accompaniment to other poultry and meats,
the marmalade can be made ahead and reheated just before serving.*

2 whole skinless and boneless duck breasts,
halved and excess fat removed
Salt and freshly ground pepper to taste
3 tablespoons unsalted butter
1/4 cup Aceto Balsamico di Modena

Onion-Balsamic Marmalade
3 tablespoons olive oil
2 large red onions, thinly sliced
1 leek, white part only, thinly sliced
1/2 cup Aceto Balsamico di Modena
1 cup chicken stock (page 106)

Preheat the oven to 375°. Lightly oil an 8-inch square baking dish.

Season the duck breasts with salt and pepper. In a large sauté pan or skillet over medium heat, melt the butter and cook until golden brown. Sear the duck breasts for 2 minutes on each side, or until lightly browned. Transfer to the prepared baking dish and sprinkle with the 1/4 cup aceto balsamico. Cover with aluminum foil and bake for 15 to 20 minutes, or until the juices run clear when the duck is pierced with a knife.

To make the marmalade: In the same sauté pan or skillet over medium heat, heat the olive oil and cook the onions and leek, stirring occa-sionally, for about 15 minutes, or until they begin to caramelize.

Add the 1/2 cup aceto balsamico, stirring to loosen the cooked bits from the bottom of the pan, and cook to reduce until syrupy. Add the chicken stock and continue to cook over medium-high heat until the liquid has reduced and the mixture is quite thick, about 10 minutes. Season with salt and pepper to taste. Set aside and keep warm.

Remove the duck breasts from the oven. Divide the onion marmalade among 4 serving plates. Arrange the duck breasts on top. Spoon the pan juices over all and serve immediately. *Serves 4*

Grilled Trout with Fresh Grape and Balsamic Sauce

Since cooked grapes are the foundation of aceto balsamico, a sauce
with a similar base is in perfect harmony.

4 whole rainbow trout (10 to 12 ounces each)
1 tablespoon olive oil
Salt and freshly ground pepper to taste
1/4 cup minced fresh mixed herbs (rosemary,
thyme, parsley)
Additional whole herb sprigs for grilling,
if desired

Grape and Balsamic Sauce
3 tablespoons extra-virgin olive oil
4 shallots, minced
1/2 cup Aceto Balsamico di Modena
2 cups vegetable stock (page 106)
2 cups red grapes, halved and
seeded if necessary

Light a fire in a charcoal grill or preheat a gas grill. Brush the trout inside and out with the olive oil. Season with salt and pepper inside and out. Sprinkle 1 tablespoon of the herbs inside each fish. Truss a couple of whole herb sprigs to each fish with kitchen string if desired. Grill until browned, about 4 minutes on each side. Place the fish on a serving platter and keep warm.

To make the sauce: In a medium saucepan, over medium heat, heat the oil and sauté the shallots until golden brown, 4 to 5 minutes. Add the aceto balsamico and stir. Add the vegetable stock and grape halves and bring to a boil. Reduce the heat and simmer for 2 minutes. Remove the grapes with a slotted spoon and set aside. Increase heat to medium-high and boil the sauce until reduced to about 1 cup. Return the grapes to the sauce. Season with salt and pepper. Spoon the sauce over and around the trout and serve immediately. *Serves 4*

Finishes

Classic Finishes

Parmigiano-Reggiano, Pear, and Aceto Balsamico Tradizionale

There is something magical about this combination: Simply arrange a wedge of Parmigiano-Reggiano, some fresh whole pears, and a bottle of Aceto Balsamico Tradizionale on a cutting board in the middle of your table. Allow your guests to chip off shards of the Parmigiano-Reggiano and drizzle it with the Aceto Balsamico Tradizionale. Fresh bites of pear interspersed with the richness of the cheese and balsamico create a culinary harmony that is hard to beat.

Fragoline di Bosco and Aceto Balsamico Tradizionale

It is not unusual to see these tiny wild strawberries growing along the bed of a woodland stream in the spring. The traditional way to serve them is drizzled with thick, aged balsamic vinegar. If you cannot find these thimble-sized jewels, substitute fresh regular strawberries, sliced and macerated with a little sugar. Use about 1 teaspoon of Aceto Balsamico Tradizionale per serving, and drizzle it on the berries just before serving.

Fresh Ricotta, Chestnut Honey, and Aceto Balsamico Tradizionale

If you can get fresh ricotta, lucky you! Slice a piece while it is still warm, or if already refrigerated, let warm to room temperature. Drizzle it with the woodsy flavor of chestnut honey and glistening droplets of Aceto Balsamico Tradizionale.

Ricotta Cheesecake with Orange Flower Water and Aceto Balsamico

*A light finish to a meal, this cheesecake is crowned with
a puddle of Aceto Balsamico Tradizionale.*

2/3 cup granulated sugar
1/3 cup all-purpose flour
30 ounces whole-milk ricotta cheese
5 egg yolks, beaten
1 tablespoon orange flower water
1/4 teaspoon freshly grated nutmeg
2 teaspoons finely grated orange zest
1 1/2 teaspoons vanilla extract
Pinch of salt
1 cup fresh orange juice
2 tablespoons Aceto Balsamico Tradizionale

Preheat the oven to 300°. Butter and lightly flour a 9-inch springform pan.

In a large bowl, combine the sugar and flour. Add the ricotta, stirring just to blend. Add the egg yolks, orange flower water, nutmeg, orange zest, vanilla, and salt.

Pour into the prepared pan and bake for 1 hour and 15 minutes, or until the top is golden brown and the cake is fairly firm (it will still be slightly soft in the center). Transfer to a wire rack and let cool. Cover and refrigerate for at least 2 hours.

In a small saucepan, cook the orange juice over high heat until reduced by half. Add the aceto balsamico and set aside to cool.

To serve, run a thin-bladed knife around the sides of the cake. Remove the pan side and cut the cake into 10 slices. Serve each slice on a serving plate with a small pool of the balsamic-orange juice sauce alongside. *Serves 10*

"WHEN MY SON WAS
YOUNG, HE GREW
TIRED OF ME SAYING
THAT ACETO
BALSAMICO COULD BE
EATEN WITH
ANYTHING. SO HE
OFFERED ME A GLASS
OF MILK AND
CHALLENGED ME TO
TRY IT WITH
BALSAMICO—IT
WASN'T BAD!"

—ERMES MALPIGHI,
MODENA

Strawberry Mousse

Rustichelli & Piccinini is a gastronomic institution. Located on the via Emilia as you enter Modena, this store belongs to a husband-and-wife team who have been sharing their culinary skills and products for thirty years. The place is a veritable museum, especially the little cupboard that houses their balsamic vinegar collection. Enoé Piccinini cooks all of the prepared foods, including this delightful strawberry pudding.

$3/4$ cup milk
$1/4$ cup confectioners' sugar
1 teaspoon vanilla extract
$1^1/2$ teaspoons plain gelatin
4 cups fresh ripe strawberries, hulled and sliced
2 tablespoons granulated sugar
$1/4$ cup twelve-year-old Aceto Balsamico Tradizionale
$3/4$ cup heavy cream

In a large saucepan, combine the milk, confectioners' sugar, vanilla, and gelatin, stirring until gelatin is dissolved. Heat over medium heat just until bubbles form around the edges of the pan. Remove from heat and let cool.

In a medium saucepan, combine the strawberries, granulated sugar, and aceto balsamico. Cook over medium heat for 10 minutes, stirring occasionally. Let cool to room temperature.

Fold half the strawberry sauce into the cooled milk mixture. Reserve the remaining sauce and refrigerate until ready to serve. In a deep bowl, whip the cream until soft peaks form. Fold the whipped cream into the strawberry-milk mixture. Turn into a 4-cup dessert mold and refrigerate for at least 3 hours, or until firm. To serve, unmold the mousse by momentarily dipping the mold into warm water. Invert onto a serving platter. Serve the remaining strawberry sauce on the side. *Serves 4*

Rolando's Pound Cake with Berry-Balsamic Sauce

Italian food and wine expert Rolando Beramendi divides his time between New York and Florence. In this recipe he has combined the best of both worlds—American pound cake and Modena's balsamic sauce for summer berries. This sauce is also delicious over vanilla gelato, panna cotta, or crème caramel.

Pound Cake
2 cups (4 sticks) unsalted butter
3 1/3 cups granulated sugar
2 teaspoons vanilla extract
10 eggs
Finely grated zest of 1 orange
4 cups cake flour
1/2 teaspoon salt

Berry-Balsamic Sauce
1 cup fresh raspberries
1 cup fresh blueberries
1 cup fresh strawberries, hulled and cut into quarters
1/2 cup twelve-year-old Aceto Balsamico Tradizionale
1/2 cup granulated sugar
2 tablespoons water

Preheat the oven to 325°. Butter two 9 x 5-inch loaf pans. Line the bottom of each pan with parchment paper and butter the paper. Lightly dust with flour, shaking out the excess.

To make the pound cake: In the bowl of an electric mixer, cream the butter until pale in color. Add the sugar and beat until fluffy. Add the vanilla. Add the eggs, one at a time, beating well after each addition. Add the orange zest, mixing well.

Add the flour by hand, stirring only enough to incorporate it; do not overmix. Pour the batter into the prepared pans and bake for 1 hour, or until a toothpick inserted in the center of each loaf comes out clean. Run a thin-bladed knife around the sides of the cake to loosen from the pan; transfer to a wire rack and let cool.

To make the sauce: In a medium saucepan, combine all the ingredients. Bring to a simmer over low heat and cook for 3 to 5 minutes, or until the berries are soft, but not completely disintegrated. Remove from heat. Serve warm over slices of pound cake. *Serves 8 to 10*

Vanilla Bean Ice Cream with Cherry-Balsamico Topping

The cherry topping is also nice with the Ricotta Cheesecake (page 98).
Other fruits can be substituted, as well—grapes are especially good.

2 cups whole milk
2 cups heavy cream
1 vanilla bean, halved lengthwise
6 egg yolks
3/4 cup granulated sugar

Cherry-Balsamico Topping
1/2 cup Aceto Balsamico di Modena
1/2 cup apple juice
1/2 cup water
1/2 cup granulated sugar
1/2 teaspoon grated lemon zest
1/2 teaspoon ground cinnamon
1 pound (about 3 cups) dark sweet cherries,
pitted and halved, or 8 ounces dried cherries

In the top of a double boiler, combine the milk and cream. Scrape the vanilla beans into the liquid, add the pod, and heat to scalding over gently boiling water. Remove from heat and set aside. Remove the vanilla pod.

In a blender, combine the egg yolks and sugar. With the machine running, slowly add the heated milk mixture. Return the mixture to the double boiler and cook over simmering water, stirring constantly, until the mixture coats the back of a wooden spoon. Let cool, then refrigerate for at least 2 hours. Then freeze in an ice cream maker according to the manufacturer's instructions.

To make the topping: In a medium saucepan, combine the aceto balsamico, apple juice, water, sugar, lemon zest, and cinnamon. Bring to a boil, stirring to dissolve the sugar. Add the cherries and decrease heat to a simmer. Cook for 8 to 10 minutes, or until the cherries are soft. Let cool to room temperature before serving. *Serves 6*

Four-Season Fruit Salad with Citrus-Balsamic Dressing

Prepare one of these combinations of fruit, or create your own mélange.
Choose ripe but firm fruit at the peak of its season when it is full of flavor.
The dressing is also delicious served on green salads and vegetables.

Citrus-Balsamic Dressing
1/2 cup orange juice
1/4 cup Aceto Balsamico di Modena
1/4 cup granulated sugar
1/2 teaspoon grated orange zest
1/4 teaspoon freshly grated nutmeg

Summer Fruit Salad
4 peaches, peeled, pitted, and sliced
1 cup fresh blueberries

Spring Fruit Salad
2 pints sweet cherries, halved and pitted
1 mango, peeled, cut from the pit, and diced

Fall Fruit Salad
12 fresh figs, quartered
1/2 cup slivered almonds, toasted (see page 107)

Winter Fruit Salad
4 pears, peeled, cored, and sliced
Seeds from 1 pomegranate

To make the dressing: In a medium saucepan, combine all the ingredients. Bring to a boil, stirring to dissolve the sugar. Remove from heat and let cool to room temperature before serving.

Toss the dressing with one of the seasonal fruit combinations and let stand at room temperature for 30 minutes before serving. *Each salad serves 4*

Pasta Dough

3 cups unbleached all-purpose flour
4 eggs
1 tablespoon safflower oil

To make with a food processor: Put the flour in a food processor fitted with the steel knife blade. In a small container with a pour spout, whisk the eggs with the oil.

With machine running, slowly add the egg mixture to the flour until the dough starts to come away from the sides of the workbowl. Process for 30 seconds and check the consistency: the dough should be moist enough to pinch together, but not sticky. On a lightly floured work surface, knead the dough several times and form a ball. Place in a plastic bag and let rest for 15 minutes.

Roll out one-fourth of the dough at a time, keeping the remaining dough in the plastic bag to avoid drying it out. Using a hand-cranked pasta maker, start on the widest setting. Put the pasta through 8 to 10 times, folding it in half each time, until the dough is smooth. If the dough tears, it may be too wet; dust it with flour, brushing off the excess.

Continue putting the dough through the rollers, but without folding it, using a narrower setting each time, until the dough is the desired thickness. Let the rolled dough dry while rolling the next piece of dough. Cut the dough into the desired pasta shape. *Makes 1 pound*

Note: To make the dough by hand, place the flour on a work surface. Make a well in the center and add the eggs and oil. With a fork, gradually blend the egg mixture into the flour. Knead by hand for 10 to 15 minutes, or until smooth and elastic.

Chicken Stock

One 3-pound chicken or chicken parts, cut up
1 carrot, peeled and cut into 1/2-inch pieces
1 stalk celery, cut into 1/2-inch pieces
1 onion, cut into 1/2-inch pieces
Bouquet garni: 1 sprig parsley, 1 bay leaf,
1 sprig thyme, 4 to 5 peppercorns
1 gallon (16 cups) water

Place all the ingredients in a large stockpot and bring to a boil.

Reduce heat to a simmer and cook uncovered for 2 hours, periodically skimming off the foam. Strain, discarding the chicken and vegetables. Refrigerate the stock until the fat solidifies and can be removed. *Makes 5 quarts*

Rich Chicken Stock: Simmer twice the amount of chicken stock as you need until the volume is reduced by half.

Roasted Chicken Stock: Place the chicken and onion in a lightly oiled baking pan. Roast in a preheated 425° oven for 20 to 25 minutes, or until browned. Continue with recipe as described above.

Vegetable Stock

1/4 cup extra-virgin olive oil
2 onions, coarsely chopped
2 carrots, peeled and coarsely chopped
3 stalks celery, coarsely chopped
1/2 cup dry white wine
1 gallon (16 cups) water
Bouquet garni: 1 sprig of parsley, 1 sprig of thyme,
1 bay leaf, 4 to 5 black peppercorns

In a large stockpot, heat the olive oil over medium heat and sauté the onion, carrots, and celery for 5 to 8 minutes, or until browned. Add the wine, increase the heat to high, and stir to loosen cooked bits from the bottom of the pan.

Continue cooking until the wine is almost completely evaporated. Add the water and bouquet garni. Bring to a boil, reduce heat to a simmer, and cook uncovered for at least 45 minutes. Strain the stock and discard the vegetables. *Makes 3 quarts*

Rich Vegetable Stock: Cook over high heat to reduce the volume by one half.

Basics

Veal Stock

10 pounds veal shank bones, cut into
3-inch lengths
2 onions, cut into 1-inch pieces
2 carrots, peeled and cut into 1-inch pieces
1 stalk celery, cut into 1-inch pieces
Bouquet garni: 1 sprig parsley, 1 bay leaf, 1 sprig
thyme, 4 to 5 peppercorns
2 gallons (32 cups) water

Preheat the oven to 425°. Put the veal bones and onions in a lightly oiled baking pan and roast for 35 to 40 minutes, or until very brown. Put the bones, onions, and all the remaining ingredients in a large stockpot and bring to a boil. Reduce heat to a simmer and cook, uncovered, for 8 hours, periodically skimming the foam from the top. Strain, discarding the solids. Refrigerate the stock until the fat solidifies and can be removed. *Makes 4 quarts*

To Toast Nuts

Put the nuts on a baking sheet and toast in a pre-heated 350° oven for 8 to 10 minutes, or until golden brown and aromatic. Pine nuts take less time, about 5 to 7 minutes.

Roasted Garlic

4 heads garlic
1/2 cup olive oil
Salt and freshly ground pepper to taste

Preheat the oven to 300°. Score around the middle of each head of garlic; do not cut into the cloves.

Remove the top half of the papery skin, exposing the cloves. Place the heads in a small oiled baking pan and pour the olive oil over them. Season with salt and pepper, cover, and bake for 1 hour. Uncover and bake for 10 to 15 minutes, basting frequently, or until the heads are very tender. Let cool.

To Peel and Seed Tomatoes

Remove the core from each tomato. Drop the tomatoes in boiling water for 30 seconds; transfer immediately to ice water to stop the cooking and release the skins. The peel will slip off in your hands. To seed, cut the tomatoes in half, invert over a sink, and squeeze out the seeds.

Resources

Mail-Order Sources

Manicaretti Imports
5332 College Avenue,
No. 200
Oakland, CA 94618
Tel. (800) 799-9830
Leonardi balsamic vinegars, artisan-quality pasta, risotto, and capers.

Dairyland U.S.A. Corporation
1300 Viele Avenue
New York, NY 10474
Tel. (718) 842-8700
Distributor for Acetaia del Cristo

DeMedici Imports
315 W. 57th Street
New York, NY 10019
Tel. (212) 974-8101
Fax (212) 581-1939
Distributor for Cavalli

Rogers International
94 Neal Street
Portland, ME 04102
Tel. (207) 879-2641
Fax (207) 879-1459
rogersin@maine.rr.com
Distributor for Acetaia Malpighi

Thinking of starting your own battery of barrels? Chef Paul Bertolli has an *acetaia* in Sonoma where he manages several batteries for local families. He is also the sole importer of Francesco Renzi's beautiful barrels from Modena.
Paul Bertolli
Oliveto Restaurant
5655 College Avenue
Oakland, CA 94618
Tel. (510) 547-5356
Fax (510) 547-4624

Worth a Visit in Italy

Emilia Romagna is an area abundant in the arts, with concerts, gallery exhibitions, and architectural wonders. Before you go, do some reading and research to take advantage of these treasures.
Tourist info: Modenatur
c/o Palazzo Municipale
Via Scudari, 8, Modena
Tel./Fax 011.39.59.20.66.86
Website: http://www.nettuno.it/fiera/cciaamo

Slow Food
Via Mendicità Istruita, 14
12042 Bra (CN)
Tel. 01139.172.41.12.73
Fax 011.39 172.42.12.93
An organization devoted to the fight against fast food. It publishes excellent guides to the gastronomic pleasures of Italy.

Consorzio di Aceto Balsamico Tradizionale di Modena
Marco Costanzini
Via Ganaceto, 134
41100 Modena
Tel. 011.39.59.23.69.81
E-mail: biancardiclaudio@agrofood.it

Consorzio fra Produttori di Aceto Balsamico Tradizionale di Reggio Emilia
Piazza della Vittoria, 1
42100 Reggio Emilia
Tel. 011.39.522.79.62.25

Consorteria di Spilamberto
Villa Fabriani
Via Roncati, 28
41057 Spilamberto (MO)
Tel./Fax 011.39.59.78.59.59

Culinary Arts: Emilia Romagna
1324 State Street, J-157
Santa Barbara, CA 93101
Tel. (805) 963-7289
Fax (805) 963-0230
E-mail: CulinarArt@aol.com
A weeklong culinary program in Emilia Romagna. Other programs also available in Piedmonte and Toscana.

List of Producers to Visit. (Please call ahead for an appointment.)

Antiche Acetaia dei Conti Guidotti Bentivoglio
Palazzo Guidotti, Corso Cavour, 60
41100 Modena
Tel. 011.39.59.23.42.83

Azienda Agricola Sante Bertoni
41040 Montegibbio di Modena (MO)
Tel. 011.39.536.87.27.78

La Ca' dal Non'
Via Zanella, 5
Vignola (MO)
Tel. 011.39.59.30.02.78

Cavalli
Via del Cristo, 6
Scandiano (RE)
Tel. 011.39.522.98.34.30

Acetaia del Cristo
Via Badia, 41, Fraz. San Lorenzo
41030 San Prospero (MO)
Tel. 011.39.59.33.03.83

Acetaia e Dispensa Leonardi
Via Mazzacavallo, 62
41010 Magreta (MO)
Tel. 011.39.59.55.43.75

Resources

Acetaia Malpighi
Via A. Pica, 310
41100 Modena
Tel. 011.39.59.28.08.93

Azienda Agricola di Italo Pedroni
Via Risaia, 2
41015 Nonantola
Tel. 011.39.59.54.90.19

Pier Luigi Sereni
Via Zenzano, 398
41054 Marano sul Panaro (MO)
Tel./Fax 011.39.59.77.21.22

Shops

Salumeria Giuseppe Giusti
Via Farini, 75
Modena
Tel. 011.39.59.22.25.33
A four-hundred-year-old purveyor of fine foods serving some of the best food in Modena (see Restaurants).

Enogastonomia Rustichelli & Piccinini
Via Emilia Est, 417
Modena
Tel. 011.39.59.36.01.19
Gourmet foods: salami, condiments, cheeses, oils, vinegars.

Enologica Modenese
Via Jugoslavia, 24
41100 Modena Nord
Tel. 011.39.59.45.05.19
Supplies for making wine, vinegar, and aceto balsamico, including delicate vials and hand-blown glass serving pieces.

Restaurants

Ristorante Lancellotti
Via Achille Grandi, 120
41019 Soliera (MO)
Tel. 011.39.59.56.74.06
Fax 011.39.59.56.54.31
Extraordinary people, serving extraordinary food, embellished with specialties from their own garden and acetaia. Also an inn. Closed Sunday and Monday.

Ristorante Francescana
Via Stella, 22
Modena
Tel. 011.39.59.21.01.18
A charming restaurant with delicious food in the center of Modena. Closed Sunday.

Osteria Giusti
Via Farini, 75
Modena
Tel. 011.39.59.22.25.33
With only four precious tables, reservations are essential to experience Laura Galli's refined handmade cooking. Lunch only. Closed Sunday.

Villa Gaidello
Via Gaidello, 18
Castelfranco Emilia (MO)
Tel. 011.39.59.92.6620
Very traditional, very homemade, and delicious. Also an inn. Closed Sunday and Monday.

Osteria di Rubbiara
Via Risaia, 2
41015 Nonantola
Tel. 011.39.59.54.90.19
Traditional Modenese home-cooked food. Be sure to clean your plate! Closed Sunday, Tuesday, and Thursday.

Picci
Via XX Settembre, 2
Cavriago (RE)
Tel. 011.39.522.37.18.01
Closed Monday and Tuesday. The Piccirilli family are also producers of aceto balsamico.

Bibliography

Anderson, Burton. *Treasures of the Italian Table.* New York: William Morrow, 1994.

Benedetti, Benedetto. *Aceto Balsamico: Manuale dell'Amatore.* Modena: Edizioni il Fiorino, 1995.

Bergonzini, Renato. *L'Aceto Balsamico: Nella Tradizione e Nella Gastonomia.* Vincenza: Mundici & Zanetti Editori, 1990.

Bergonzini, Renato. *In Cucina con l'Aceto Balsamico.* Bologna: Mundici & Zanetti Editori, 1996.

Cavazzuti, Vittorio. *Aceto Balsamico: Tradizione e Use di un Antico e Pregiato Condimento.* Fiesole: Nardini Editore, 1994.

Consorzio Tutela Aceto Balsamico di Modena. *L'Aceto Balsamico di Modena.* Savignano s.P. (MO): Litografia F.G.

Kasper, Lynne Rossetto. *The Splendid Table: Recipes from Emilia-Romagna, the Heartland of Northern Italian Food.* New York: William Morrow, 1992.

Plotkin, Fred. *Italy for the Gourmet Traveler.* Little, Brown, 1996.

Sacchetti, Mario. *L'Aceto Balsamico Modenese.* Bologna: Edagricole-Edizioni Agricole, 1991.

Salvaterra, Gianni. *L'Aceto Balsamico Tradizionale di Modena.* Bologna: Calderini, 1994.

General Index

Recipe Index

Acknowledgments

Pamela Sheldon Johns would like to thank the following: Courtney, Alaia, Lucy, and Toby Johns for all of their sweetness and love.

Marco Constanzini, for his help in understanding the legal issues, and also for helping me get my car out of tow-truck hell; and Jane Calabria McPeak, for interpretation and friendly assistance.

For support and friendship: Kimberly Wicks Bartolozzi, Rolando Beramendi, Francesca Cantini, Ed Valenzuela, and Sara Wilson.

For visits to *acetaie:* Erika and Eugenio Barbieri; Otello Bonfatti; Roberto and Giovanni Cavalli; Clara and Giovanni Leonardi; Ermes Malpighi; Mariangela, Vittorio, and Michele Montanari; Francesco, and Maura Renzi; Pier Luigi Sereni; and Valeriano Zanasi.

For feeding me well: Paola Bini, Massimo Bottura, the Lancellotti family, the Montanari family, Nano and Laura Morandi, and Italo Pedroni.

For testing recipes: Gioia Bartoli, Mari Bartoli, Judy Dawson, Nancy Edney, Philippa Farrar, Paula Ferguson, Linda Hale, Diana Harris, and Joan Willicombe.

And for a wonderful collaboration, I thank Jennifer Barry and Richard Jung, Lorena Jones, Kirsty Melville, Cynthia Traina, and Dennis Hayes.

Jennifer Barry Design would like to acknowledge the following individuals and establishments for their help and support on this book project:

Special thanks to Kirsty Melville and Lorena Jones of Ten Speed Press for their continued support and enthusiasm for great Italian food.

Pamela Sheldon Johns for another wonderful collaborative experience and for introducing us to Aceto Balsamico Tradizionale, which has changed our eating habits forever!

Richard Jung for travelling to Modena and capturing "the beauty in the attics" of the vinegar-making process that we may all now enjoy in this book. For this, in addition to his lovely photography of the recipes, with the help of stylist Pouké , we are most appreciative.

Tom Johnson, Leslie Barry, Kristen Wurz, Maria Hjelm, Carolyn Miller, and Barbara King for their continuing expert assitance in producing the book.

The photography and styling team would like to thank photographic assistant Ivy, assistant food stylist Karen Wang, background artist Michelle Syracuse. From Draeger's Market, San Mateo thanks to Matt Buckman, Specialty Food Department, and Josette Selim and Nancy Gentry, Top of the Market Department. Thanks also to Barbara Chambers/Spencer House, San Francisco, and to Juliet and Helena, for their support.